LOCKING DOWN THE POOR

ALSO BY HARSH MANDER IN SPEAKING TIGER

Looking Away: Inequality, Prejudice and Indifference in New India
Fatal Accidents of Birth: Stories of Suffering, Oppression and Resistance

LOCKING DOWN THE POOR

The Pandemic and India's Moral Centre

HARSH MANDER

SPEAKING
TIGER

SPEAKING TIGER BOOKS LLP
4381/4, Ansari Road, Daryaganj
New Delhi 110002

First published by Speaking Tiger Books in paperback in 2021

ISBN: 978-93-89958-75-1
eISBN: 978-93-89958-76-8

10 9 8 7 6 5 4 3 2 1

Typeset in Adobe Garamond Pro by SŪRYA
Printed at Pragati Printers, New Delhi

CONTENTS

1

Hunger

'I won't die of Corona. Before that I will die of hunger.'

I am in Old Delhi with a group of young friends, volunteers of Aman Biradari's Karwan-e-Mohabbat campaign, trying to feed homeless people in a small, almost helpless gesture of solidarity. It is only the third day after Prime Minister Modi announced a countrywide lockdown in a bid to contain the COVID-19 pandemic, and I have heard these words spoken more than a dozen times already. Through the dire weeks and months that are to follow, I will hear them repeated hundreds of times.

On an oppressively hot afternoon in April 2020, about two weeks after the lockdown was imposed, our food van is in Kashmere Gate, parked near the now-deserted interstate bus terminal. A young man with his face wrapped in a white handkerchief is awaiting his turn to receive the meal we are serving. He erupts in rage: 'The government is asking us to stay inside our homes. Does it expect us to break the walls and eat the pieces?' When he reaches the head of the queue, he is shaking, and he breaks down as he accepts the khichdi and pickle.

It is evident by now that India has plunged deep into what will probably be the greatest humanitarian crisis that most of us, barring those who lived through Partition and the Bengal Famine of 1943, have seen in our lifetime. But there are many who still don't see that the devastating crisis has been brought about but not *created* by the COVID-19 pandemic. The crisis is, in fact, the direct consequence of public policy choices that the union government has made. Particularly the decision to impose the most stringent lockdown on the planet without notice on the *entire* country—a country the size of a continent which is home to the largest number of people living in extreme poverty and ranks 102 out of 117 in the Global Hunger Index; a country with an unemployment rate of over 24% and 92% of its labour-force comprising informal workers; and a country with some of the lowest spending in the world on public health and social security.

Literally within days of the overnight closure of the country's economy, we begin to see signs of mass hunger, visible first in the cities: people spending humiliating hours in queues, sometimes stretching over two kilometres, for a ladle of very basic, often cold food;[1] dazed and desperate women and men, even children, rushing down empty roads—unmindful of the 'curfew' and enduring police lathis—whenever there is news or rumour of food being distributed somewhere.[2] I remember seeing such scenes decades back as a district officer, but even then only rarely, during famine-like droughts in the countryside. I have never seen anything like this in a city.

As my colleagues and I walk the streets of Delhi to offer food and dry ration packs to as many people as we can, it becomes apparent that hunger has deluged the Indian capital. Hundreds of thousands are diminished and depleted by a gnawing, constant longing for a full stomach, and the shame of not being able to feed those they love. This is a torment and humiliation that people who have not experienced involuntary hunger can never know.

The first to be swept away by this entirely human-made flood of hunger are the city's homeless. Their devastation is almost immediate, because most of them have no savings or stores of food to tide them over a single day. Barely 72 hours into the lockdown, the Karwan-e-Mohabbat van drives with cooked food to a street corner in Company Bagh. Situated between the Old Delhi Railway Station and the Chandni Chowk Town Hall, this is a 'labour adda'. Here, on any ordinary morning, you will find gathered maybe a thousand homeless men and some women offering their services for casual work to anyone, practically on any terms—they are desperate for work and powerless to bargain for a decent daily wage. Since the lockdown their numbers have swelled many times, and now include the newly homeless—those who could earlier afford dormitories or shared single rooms on rent. People squat on the pavement and at the edge of the road as far as the eye can go. A young man says to us, 'I haven't seen a roti for four days. And to think that I earned my living making rotis in a tandoor. Most days I would earn five or six hundred rupees. Today I'm waiting for hours for your khichdi.'

There are many skilled workmen like him in the food queue, he says. The word he uses is '*karigar*', artisan. Several other voices join his, speaking of their work in dhabas, small restaurants and roadside food stalls, and now the irony and agony of their hunger. Daily-wage workers, whose existence is always precarious, for whom insecurity and hardship are daily realities, also don't remember a time when things were this calamitous. If nothing else, with their passage to the city they had at least escaped hunger. Or so they thought, until the lockdown. 'We have no family here, no aadhar card, just our hands to work with,' a daily-wager tells us. 'We would work hard all day and collect three-four hundred rupees, we would sleep on the streets. But we didn't starve. We found work most days and we managed to send money home. What are we to do now, when all work has been snatched from us?'

They often name the prime minister in their helplessness and wrath. 'Why has Modi ji done this to us? If we are hungry, will we not be more at risk of catching the disease?'

Some young men rush to steady an elderly blind man. Even in normal times he survives on alms; he looks bewildered and utterly defeated now. A woman approaches us, holding her small baby. She was returning to her village in Bihar when trains were suddenly cancelled the night the lockdown was announced. Strangers—a family in a shack near the railway station—took pity on her and gave her food. 'But how long can I depend on them?' she says. 'They are also without work and food.'

Yamuna Pushta is a stretch of land on the banks of the Yamuna river, adjacent to the Nigambodh cremation ground. Usually there are about 4000 homeless men who live here. In the early days of the lockdown, we see their numbers rise to well over 10,000, as the homeless from other locations and stranded migrants converge here in the hope that food charities will reach them because of the large numbers. A legendary Sardar ji (who insists on remaining anonymous) has fed a few thousand homeless people in the area every single day for the last 15 years. Even he is shocked and overwhelmed by the level of hunger he suddenly encounters now.

The lines are far longer at the Pushta than at Company Bagh. The men squat in a line, bodies pressed against each other, their manifest desperation making a mockery of the mindless official platitude of 'social distancing'. The rumour of food being supplied somewhere is enough to spark a near-stampede as men fall over each other to reach the spot. Very often the old and the disabled among them are left far behind, empty-handed, empty-bellied.

In Nizamuddin Basti, home to thousands of families living on the streets, people tell us that their food stores and

All photos in the book by Sandeep Yadav.

money are exhausted. Children crying for milk are given tepid black tea. A woman says, 'If we eat the little that we have at night, there is no food in the morning. If there is food in the morning, there's nothing at night. We try to kill our hunger with tea. But a glass of tea costs ten rupees, four of us share it between ourselves.'

And here again we encounter helpless, powerless rage. 'How can we survive without work, you tell me? They are killing the poor like dogs,' a man cries. An old man hobbles up to us. 'I was begging at a traffic light,' he says, 'I was hungry, and also longing for a cup of tea. But the police beat me with their lathis. Do you see the blood on my pyjamas? This is what they are doing to us.'

*

The settlements of the homeless are only the first to experience mass hunger in Delhi. Soon after, the tide of hunger has reached the 'unauthorised' slums that are crunched up between middle-class enclaves across the metropolis.

One day in the middle of April our food van is in Majnu ka Tila, north Delhi. As I walk past a shanty of bamboo and plastic sheets, a woman cooking outside over a fire of twigs in a brick *chullah* hurriedly covers the vessel with the edge of her frayed sari. 'I'm ashamed,' she explains simply when I ask. She feels disgraced that she's cooking the feet of chicken, which are usually thrown away as waste. 'What can we do when there is no money?' I sit on the ground beside her and try to tell her that it is not she who should be ashamed but the government which has driven her to this. She's doing all she can to feed her family, she should hold her head high. But even as I say these words, I wonder what they can mean to her at a time of such trial.

Another woman suddenly breaks down as she speaks to us. 'We heard someone was distributing food at the school. We ran there, but by the time our turn came there was no food left. They only gave us two bananas.' She turns her face away to hide her tears. 'Come into my home and see for yourself. The stove is cold, it hasn't been used for many days. There's nothing to cook.'

In this crowded slum littered with broken glass, bits of plastic and rotting waste, most people survive in normal times by carving *silbattas*—grinding stones—and the others by pulling cycle rickshaws, or by rag-picking or working as domestic help. All of this was halted overnight. Some of the children, desperate and hungry, gather at the traffic lights to beg but they are driven away by the police. In any case, when the whole city is locked down, who is there to beg from?

The situation is no different in the shanties in the shadow of Tughlakabad fort. Here, families go from house to house bartering vessels in exchange for old clothes. Some of them supplement the meagre family income by rag-picking, and a few of the older people by begging. A young woman with a listless baby at her hip speaks into the camera held by one of my young colleagues who is interviewing people affected by the lockdown. She addresses Prime Minister Modi and Chief Minister Kejriwal. 'Is this the state you want to reduce us to?' she asks them piercingly. Another woman says, 'We fear we are fated to die. They say this Corona illness will go on for a year. They will later say we died of Corona, but actually we would have died of hunger.'

Residents of both settlements tell us that as summer is peaking, drinking water is becoming as scarce as food. There has never been water supply of any kind in either settlement, not even a public tap. In Majnu ka Tila they usually carry water in plastic containers from outside an apartment building a kilometre away, and in Tughlakabad they beg the driver of the tanker that comes to water the trees lining the main avenue for some water. This has become near impossible now; the police chase them back, often thrashing them with their lathis for violating 'Modi ji's curfew'. Bathing even occasionally has become a challenge, and washing hands frequently, of course, was out of the question even before the lockdown. In usual times they would pay ten rupees in the morning and five in the non-peak afternoons at the Sulabh Complex every time they needed to bathe or defecate. Now, when they don't have money even for food, this too is impossible. They are forced to relieve themselves in the open.

The deluge of hunger breaks into many other parts of the metropolis. The Karwan volunteers are overwhelmed by distress calls round the clock, from every corner of the city, and soon from across the country. Our phone helpline begins to get jammed with calls from industrial areas around Delhi. The winding lines of people who gather to receive our ration kits in these areas mostly comprise factory workers, both men and women, employed in micro and small industrial units making shoes, chappals, jeans, machine parts and a surprising range of other products. Work was more or less regular and secure before the lockdown, although few, if any, had written contracts or were paid the statutory minimum wage. Now the factories are all shut. A few employers have paid them for the month of March, but almost none beyond that—with no sales, most employers don't have the capacity, even if they had the will, to pay. Landlords are pressing the workers for rent. The starving workers do not blame their landlords. Many are not much wealthier than them, and critically depend on the rental income from the hole-in-the wall rooms that they let out. The workers speak to us of the anguish of children without milk, and the ignominy of lining up for food for several hours each day.

An out-of-work maali asks, 'Does the government really believe it is dangerous to step outside? Then it must want us to die. Has the government even tried to bring food to our jhuggi? The rich can have packed hot food delivered to their door. We must walk long distances and stand on the road for hours with a hundred, two hundred others.' He is not wrong. In the long queues for every cooked meal, as in the hopelessly overcrowded school buildings in which tens of thousands of migrant workers prevented from returning home are being incarcerated, the virus, locked out of middle-class homes, will flourish and multiply, transported rapidly from one underfed body to another.

Everywhere we travel, we are engulfed by complaints of inadequate and poorly cooked food—undercooked rice and watery dal, almost always cold. And rice in any case is not the staple of many people in North India. Food also often runs out as lines stretch for a kilometre or more, leading to despair and frustration, frayed tempers and sometimes small stampedes. Some workers tell us that their landlords threaten to evict them if they go out of their rooms to queue up for food, for fear that they will bring back infections.

Food relief groups like the Karwan team quickly learn that what is most useful and least undignified is to assemble dry packets of rice, flour, dal, oil, masala and soap to last a family or group of five at least ten days, and this is what we then begin to distribute. We learn; but the governments don't.

Our volunteers also get calls from collectives of sex workers about how work has completely dried up. Many home-based sex workers are migrants from other states and do not have ration cards or aadhar cards with a Delhi address, therefore they are excluded from state assistance. They speak about begging shopkeepers for rations on credit and the men expecting sexual favours in return. Several survive only with the ration kits we are able to supply every ten days.

Belatedly, the Delhi government announces that e-coupons would be issued to those without ration cards. But, as we will see in the later pages of this book, this requires both a smartphone and proof of a Delhi address, thus excluding both the vulnerable and the migrants—the very people the scheme was meant to include.

*

It is true that even before the lockdown hunger was not unknown in India's cities. For homeless people, as for old people without care-givers and disabled people without personal support systems, there is never a time when hunger is not just a heartbeat away, even in a metropolis like Mumbai or Delhi or Bengaluru. But most times it is kept at bay. If you are willing to do any work at all, even the most humiliating, unprotected, exploitative work—manually cleaning or sorting waste, pulling rickshaws, doing daily-wage or casual-sex work—at least subsistence-level employment is mostly at hand. When even that fails, there are gurudwaras, dargahs and temples where you can get some food to stay alive.

It is this everyday reality of urban India that the lockdown altered so calamitously.

While India has not been releasing health and nutrition figures since 2014, data from 2011-12 confirms that even in normal times the lowest ends of city populations are barely a step away from starvation.[3] It is widely accepted that the lower threshold of thc average daily consumption of energy necessary for a healthy individual is 2,160 kilo calories. Studies from 2011-12 showed that in 59% of the bottom five per cent and 47% of the next five per cent of India's urban households, individuals did not manage even this minimum calorie intake. The result has been widespread malnutrition: according to a 2015 report, almost ten lakh—a million—children in Delhi suffered stunted growth from malnutrition.[4] The only official report on nutrition released by the BJP-led NDA government, the National Health and Family Survey 2015-16, shows that 31% of urban children under five years of age are malnourished and 29% are underweight. An analysis of the National Family Health Surveys conducted between 2006 and 2016 revealed 1.5 to 1.8 times higher prevalence of thinness, short stature and moderate to severe anaemia among urban poor women compared with averages for urban women in general. The data demonstrated that 'among urban poor mothers, 12.8% were short, 20.6% were thin (3.5% being severely thin), 13.7% were overweight, 21.1% were obese, 57.4% had any anaemia, and 32.4% had moderate to severe anaemia'.[5]

This means that a huge segment of India's urban poor—casual workers, homeless people and residents of slums—were already living at the edge of hunger when the lockdown was imposed, shattering the economy and their livelihoods. The government can hardly claim it was ignorant of the reality of these dispossessed people.

*

Hunger soon spreads to India's smaller towns and the countryside.

Just outside the district town of Nuh bordering the 'Millennial City' Gurgaon, recently renamed Gurugram, are a number of settlements of near-destitute families who live in flimsy shelters put together with plastic sheets and bamboo. In one of these jhuggis lives Shahnaz, who has been raising her children alone since her husband died a few years ago, shortly after they moved to Nuh from their village in Bihar. Shahnaz works as domestic help, sweeping floors and cleaning dishes. But all of that work dried up on the morning of 25th March. Her eldest son, still in his teens, had also begun to earn for the family with the sweat of casual daily wage labour. That too stopped. 'We never made enough to save anything, we live from day to day,' Shahnaz tells us. Every day the family waits for the cooked food that some people—she does not know who, whether the administration or citizen groups—supply. But the supply is irregular, and with the growing summer heat, the food is sometimes spoiled by the time it reaches them, usually around noon.

In another jhuggi lives Mansoor Ali with his family. Trying to escape a life of desperate poverty in their village in Assam's Barpeta district, they had reached Nuh with the help of some relatives about five years ago. There are very few means of making some kind of living available to those for whom most pathways are blocked because of India's million exclusions. One of these is waste recycling, and this is what Ali and his family turned to. His wife and children scour the garbage dumps and streets of Nuh and surrounding areas for anything that can be recycled and sold—plastic, glass, metal. They do not earn much, but it was enough to survive, until the lockdown.

Now when they go out to look for and sift waste, the police beat them back with sticks and batons. However, even if they were able to dodge the police and somehow reach the waste heaps, what use would that be? The waste contractors who buy their waste have all had to close their shops. The family don't have ration cards. They have received no rations, indeed no support at all from the government. Some citizen groups help out with cooked food once a day. Apart from that, there is nothing.

Among other residents of the settlements surrounding Nuh is Suban. His extended family occupies four adjacent plastic-sheet jhuggis by the side of a road. They are from a nomadic community which traces its origins to Chittor in Rajasthan. In their own folklore, they believe that they are descendants of the fabled king Maharana Pratap. Their lived reality, however, is as distant as can be from a king's. Criminalized since colonial times, people of this community traditionally travel from place to place in search of work, always dodging the police. They are hereditary lohars or ironsmiths, adept at repairing iron farm instruments and knives. Three years earlier, their travels had brought them to the district of Nuh. They found work here, and the local people allowed them to settle in the outskirts of the district town. Before the lockdown they would walk from village to village, and were able to find enough work to feed their families. When the lockdown was imposed, it was the time of the year when the wheat crop is harvested. They wait the entire year for this period because there is a high demand for their services, to sharpen and repair harvesting instruments. But this year it has been the worst of times. The police, Suban says, won't let them move anywhere on the road. 'They are doing their duty,' he adds quickly. 'They have to prevent the spread of the disease, we understand that. But what do they expect us to do when we have to watch our children go to sleep with their stomachs empty?'

*

I travel to western Assam to join my young friend Abdul Kalam Azad who is leading a team of Karwan-e-Mohabbat volunteers organizing food relief in rural Assam. I meet Marjina Begum in a village not far from the headquarters of Barpeta district. In her fifties, she thinks of herself as old. Her poor health has made her infirm and physically weak; but the weight and urgency of her responsibilities keep her moving; she cannot afford to rest. For fourteen years now she has lived in the state capital, Guwahati, where she works full-time as a domestic helper with a single family, for which she is paid four thousand rupees a month and given two meals a day.

She toils well over ten hours every day so that she can raise and educate her daughter, and support her teenaged son and ailing mother. Her routine is unchanging: 'I eat in the house where I work. I eat in the afternoon, then again at night and after that come home to sleep.' Out of the four thousand rupees she earns, she spends two thousand to pay the house rent where she lives with her son. With her small income, she couldn't afford an education for him in the city. He worked as a rag-picker for some time, then apprenticed in a garage, and is now learning carpentry. The daughter lives with the grandmother and studies in the village school.

When the lockdown was imposed Marjina was in the village, visiting her mother and daughter. It has been weeks of uncertainty since then. She tells me they have no agricultural land; the green fields surrounding her village home belong to her neighbours. They have all sown paddy, but are struggling to get water for their fields during the lockdown. 'But Allah took mercy, he has showered rain.' When her neighbours bring the crop home, she hopes that her small family, too, will be able to survive. 'No one here will eat full meals while their neighbour starves. They will spare some food grain for those who don't have any.' But no matter how generous the neighbours are, the grain won't last long.

Marjina herself has mastered the art of going hungry for days. She has known hunger and abject poverty since she was an infant. During her childhood, river floods would destroy the crop of the entire village and they would struggle for months in famine-like conditions. She says to me, 'We have lived through difficult times. We cooked gruel with a handful of wheat flour and it was all we ate through the day. We survived.' So she believes that people will suffer terribly but they won't die of hunger so easily. Allah will help them get through this crisis. But she is saddened that her children may have to endure the torment of hunger if the lockdown continues much longer. Her entire life has been about protecting them from this torment, she never wanted them to experience what she did as a child. That she may now fail to do so keeps her awake at night.

Like Marjina, Rahizuddin, a 45-year-old tenant farmer of Bhokowamari village in Baksa district, cannot sleep at night. 'I am in tension all the time,' he says to us dispiritedly. We watch the shadows pass over his face on our phone screens during the video-call we make to him with the help of friends engaged in relief work in his district. 'I cannot eat,' he says. 'I cannot sleep. I just keep thinking about the future and it frightens me terribly.'

This promised to be a good farming year before the calamity hit without any warning. Rahizuddin owns no land, and each year he takes on lease three bighas (0.4 hectares) of farmland from a bigger landlord of his village. The terms of the lease commit him to pay the landowner 18,000 rupees regardless of the fate of the harvest. The rest of the earnings are his, as are all investments and of course any losses. This year he cultivated perishable vegetables like bitter gourd, ridge gourd, cucumber and radish. The crop had been good. He hoped to sell his produce in the market and bring in at least 50,000 rupees. Even after he paid the landlord his share, there would be enough for his family, and he would have some money left over to invest in his next paddy cultivation. But then, 'just like that', without warning, the complete lockdown was announced. He had heard that an epidemic had broken out, some disease that everyone was talking about, so everyone was prohibited from moving out of their homes for three weeks. Helplessly, his heart sinking, he had watched his harvest rot. His family ate some of the vegetables, they shared some with their neighbours, and fed some to the cows. But most of it just decomposed and putrefied.

His 'tension' (he uses the English word) is for many reasons. Even though he won't earn a single rupee now, he will still have to pay the landlord the agreed share, otherwise the landlord won't lease him the land in future. To pay the landlord, Rahizuddin will have to take a loan from the local moneylender, at very high interest rates. He will also have to find money for his next harvest, which is already due. Nor is he sure when the government will allow him to work his fields again. How will he feed his family?

*

The horror, torment and indignity of hunger, even in a pandemic, even during a lockdown, is entirely preventable. To save its people from this preventable suffering is the most elementary duty of the state. But at a time of one of the gravest crises in the country's history, the Indian state has been adrift. Bereft of vision, administrative capacity and public compassion.

2

Dispensable Lives

The privileged Indian has for too long been comfortable with some of the most unconscionable inequalities on the planet. In its response to the COVID-19 pandemic, the Indian government aligned itself entirely with this India of privilege. The lockdown exacerbated the already deep fractures in Indian society, as it destroyed the fragile livelihoods of the most marginalized people, leaving them exposed to disease and greater destitution, not only for the present but, I believe, for years to come.

It was common knowledge that the virus had no cure and its spread could only be prevented. The first measures adopted by the government to slow its dispersal were to advise people to work from home, wash their hands frequently and maintain '*do gaj ki doori*', a distance of two yards. All of these were measures that only people of some means could adopt. For the rest—over half the country's population—the government had no plan.

And then, abruptly, through a dramatic primetime 'address to the nation' of the kind that he so favours, Prime Minister Narendra Modi announced a countrywide lockdown late on the evening of 24th March. In a decree reflecting unbridled hubris, he gave the billion and a quarter Indian people just three and a half hours' notice before shutting them into their homes and enforcing the closure—unprecedented in human history in its scale and audacity—of the entire economy and all transport. The prime minister spoke of this as a 21-day war during which the virus would be conquered. Subsequently, he extended the lockdown thrice, right up to 31st May, after which his government announced the gradual nationwide unlocking of economic activity and partial lifting of curfew measures. Six months later, as I write this, the pandemic continues to rage across the country, and the economy remains shattered.

Public health experts, as we shall see, are divided about whether the extreme measure of a complete lockdown was ever necessary or indeed implementable. But it should have been obvious from the start that a total lockdown could, even in theory, ensure safety only to those with assured incomes or savings, homes with spaces for distancing (or homes of any kind at all), regular power supply and running water, in-house toilets and the resources to buy and store essential items in bulk. This would have been possible for maybe 40 crore Indians. For the remaining 90 crore, there would be no protection from the virus, only the unbearable burden of the costs of the lockdown. Then how can any administration justify the choice of this strategy which might arguably protect the privileged and relatively privileged classes but which in its very design entirely excludes, and often imperils, the dispossessed?

Exclusion and a shocking reinforcing of inequalities was evident from the very beginning in the responses of the government and much of civil society to the pandemic. The government, for example, did nothing to clearly and firmly reject or even discourage the use of the term 'social distancing', which is an unfortunate idea in the Indian context. Caste is an extreme and inhuman form of social distancing that we have practiced for millennia. Indeed, 'social distancing' mimics many age-old caste prohibitions: keeping distance, refusing to touch, not sharing utensils, denying entry into one's home. Which probably explains why the practice was adopted by the majority of privileged Indians with such ease. Politicians, policy makers, scientists, journalists, celebrity artistes, business leaders—every popular public figure, almost without exception, used the phrase and promoted the practice over and over again, all of them unmindful of the fact that they were thus further normalizing a civilizational apartheid.

It isn't surprising, then, that the Modi administration decided to abandon the poor and the disadvantaged and choose a strategy which even its proponents regard as only partially effective, and suitable for high-income rather than developing countries. When ordering the lockdown, did the union government not remember the vast majority of Indians who would have no earnings if they stayed at home? These include nine out of every ten labourers who work in the informal economy, casual daily-wagers who search for work every day, self-employed people like rag-pickers, rickshaw-pullers, mechanics and street vendors and people forced to survive on alms. Many of these people are also circular migrants. A large number are elderly people and people with disabilities without any support systems, to whom the state provides little or no social security.

The Azim Premji University's *State of Working India* report of 2018 estimates that 85% of India's workforce earn less than Rs 10,000 a month; in fact, 50% of the workforce earn less than Rs 5,000 a month. The lockdown abruptly snapped even this income. Small and medium enterprises shut down, and construction and informal workplaces like eateries and tailoring units all closed. The lockdown resulted swiftly in an estimated 11.4 crore (114 million) job losses—over nine crore daily-wage earners and almost two crore salary earners have been laid off across 271,000 factories and 6.5 to 7 crore small and micro enterprises.[6] Even at the best of times many of these workers earn barely enough to feed and clothe themselves and their families. Their savings are meagre, and the daily wagers among them have none. Did the government expect them to voluntarily starve for the 'larger good' of preventing the spread of the infection?

When the prime minister sagely advised his fellow citizens to practice 'social distancing' and 'self-isolation', and asked them to treat the threshold of their homes as a 'Lakshman

rekha', a sacred line not to be crossed, he was manifestly indifferent to the living reality of hundreds of thousands of children, women and men in every single Indian city who have no home to stay back in; for whom the only home is the pavement or a dirt patch under some bridge or flyover. The 2011 census estimated that India has 17 lakh, or 1.7 million, homeless people. Those of us who work with the homeless recognize that they are hard to count. We estimate that there are at least 30 lakh urban homeless adults in India and additionally at least half that number of street children, all of them undernourished and vulnerable to disease and illness. Homeless men, we have found, are particularly vulnerable to tuberculosis, which puts them at greater risk of death if infected with COVID-19. Like all homeless people, they had no option during the lockdown but to sleep in overcrowded, unsanitary government shelters or quarantine centres, which are veritable breeding grounds for every deadly infection, including COVID-19.

The prime minister also forgot that this is the fate of people in beggars' homes as well, and of prisoners in our notoriously overcrowded jails. And of course, how could he have acknowledged the dangers to the lives of the unfortunate people confined to detention centres in Assam, which I have personally seen—jails within jails; places any civilized person would call hell.

The prime minister was also not mindful of the fact that even among those with some kind of homes to live in, the 'do gaj ki doori' that he advocated is possible only for a small segment of people. Let us assume, conservatively, that a household of five (which is the average size of an Indian household, according to government data[7]) would need a house of at least two middle-sized rooms and a separate kitchen for adequate physical distancing. The room-wise housing data from the 2011 census of India indicates that a staggering 67% of urban dwellers live in houses with two or less rooms and no separate kitchen. Even by our conservative assumption, then, about two-thirds of India's urban population was in no position to maintain physical distancing when the lockdown was imposed. The same census tells us that five people share a single room in four out of every ten Indian families, and that for almost ten crore households home is just a single room—where five people, if not more, sleep, cook, eat and sleep.[8] We must also not forget that these were the numbers in 2010-11, they would be higher in 2020.

How is physical distancing feasible for large extended families or collectives of several single male migrants living in narrow single rooms in slums and working-class tenements? In a survey for the India Exclusion Report 2020-21 (not yet published), researcher-activists Reetika Revathy Subramanian and Sanjay Patel of the Aajeevika Bureau describe the lives of migrant men from Odisha's Ganjam district who work as loom workers in Gujarat's Surat city, India's textile capital. Even before the COVID-19 pandemic rendered them unemployed and stranded, pushing them to the edge of starvation, their daily lives were of unrelenting toil and precarity. Yet, an unending supply of workers desperate to take their place meant that they endured their lot. These men work in shifts, and between shifts nearly 60 of them must fit into a 500-square-feet room, colloquially referred to as 'mess rooms', where they sleep on worn-out mattresses sometimes infested with bedbugs. The mess rooms have two toilets at one end that all the occupants use. The water for bathing, drinking and cooking comes from a common source. The lockdown left them devastated. When the power looms pulled down their shutters, the Odia weavers told Subramaniam and Patel, they were forced to stay indoors all day and all night. The poorly ventilated mess rooms now had to accommodate *both* shifts of workers at once: over 100 workers were packed inside each 500-square-feet room, fearing for their lives and sanity.

Their predicament is not exceptional; this is how dire things were for almost all of India's working poor. How, indeed, is physical distancing possible for someone like Mofidul, an embroidery worker who migrated to Delhi from Bengal in 2003 and lives in Shahpur Jat, one of Delhi's 'urban villages', sharing a 15x12 feet dormitory with 18 other workers? Or for Sampath, also a migrant from West Bengal, staying in a 6x6 feet room with five other casual workers?[9] Or for Kanhaiya, sharing a room with four other daily wagers in a building in a slum cluster in south-west Delhi's Kapashera; an overcrowded building, with a single common toilet per floor, where as many as 58 people had tested positive for COVID-19?[10] Across the country, tens of millions of migrant workers like Mofidul, Sampath and Kanhaiya, often far from their loved ones, risked infection, disease and starvation and battled crushing anxiety and depression through the terrible days of the lockdown.

Even for families with a home, can an entire family stay locked-in for two months in a tiny shanty with no running water and a community toilet catering to 100 people or more? Take Mumbai, for instance, the country's largest and wealthiest city. Over 60 lakh—by some estimates, nearly a crore—of its residents live in slums. Just 30 sq km of the city's total habitable area is available to them. The average density of the slums is 2000 persons (approximately 400 tenements) per hectare, and the health and environmental conditions are appalling: there is no access to safe drinking water, the sewage network is almost non-existent, the common toilets rarely have water connections, and there are piles of garbage in sunless lanes so narrow that no more than two people can walk side by side. Typically, six to ten people live in shifts in the 80- to 100-square-feet one-room tenements. But during the lockdown, they were all forced to crowd themselves into these dim, airless spaces for days and months.[11]

Recorded messages on phones urging citizens to wash their hands frequently must seem like a cruel joke to these people, especially when governments make no special arrangements to bring them adequate water even during a pandemic. As public health experts at WaterAid India have recorded, 'Most informal settlements rely on tanker-based water supply in the absence of piped water. During the lockdown, even tankers have become either unavailable or intermittent, forcing people to walk long distances to fetch water. Added to this is the challenge of the inevitable chaos that happens when [a] tanker reaches slums, where people crowd around the tankers out of desperation.'[12] By a conservative estimate, a person would need about two litres of water for a single thorough hand wash with soap; which would mean eight litres to wash hands even four times a day. A family of five—the average size of an urban Indian family—would thus need 40 litres a day just to wash their hands. How is this possible for slum-dwellers who buy a pot of water sometimes for a fifth of their day's earnings (irregular incomes, further decimated by the lockdown).

Town planners Hussain Indorewala and Shweta Wagh remind us that by refusing to learn lessons from history, we put the lives of the working poor at immense risk in times of epidemics. The COVID-19 pandemic is not a crisis of the city, they say, but the crisis of a *certain kind* of city. Between 1896 and 1899, a deadly bubonic plague killed 44,984 people in Bombay, with poorer neighbourhoods the worst hit. Urban planners emphasised then that the answer to insanitation was light and air, 'nature's two great healing elements which everyone might have *gratis ad libitum* if public opinion insisted on every dwelling room having sufficient open space about it'. Today Ratan Tata laments the 'miserable standard of living in slums with lack of fresh air, hygiene, open space', but the neo-liberal policies that are hailed so insistently by people like him led to the private sector being invited to produce housing for the poor, which has now resulted in public health regulations being diluted to make urban development projects 'viable', squeezing people into smaller and smaller areas and packing buildings closer than ever before. The government and builders have become facilitators and spectators of human misery.[13]

Every medical expert will tell us that to avoid catching an infection, we should avoid crowded indoor spaces. This has been proven and accepted common sense for well over a century. So when the Indian state forced the poor into cramped rooms or makeshift shelters, denying them fresh air, natural light and the chance to feed themselves adequately and with dignity—indeed, denying them all agency—it clearly endangered their lives. There is greater, constant crowding in these spaces than outdoors, and the spread not only of COVID-19 but also of other contagious diseases with much higher mortality rates like tuberculosis becomes far more likely. On 7 April 2020, just a fortnight into India's lockdown, researchers released a study conducted over two months in 320 Chinese cities which showed that an overwhelming majority of the COVID-19 infections were transmitted indoors. The six researchers, from the Southeast University in Nanjing, the University of Hong Kong and the University of Beijing, concluded that 'sharing indoor space is a major SARS-CoV-2 infection risk'.[14] This should have made governments and civil society re-assess the strategy of closing all open public spaces (rather than regulating them to prevent crowding) especially in areas where large numbers of people live in densely populated slums or substandard buildings. This did not happen, and stringent lockdowns continued in many countries across the world, the most mindlessly stringent of these in India.

'Why has the lockdown solution become so entrenched?' asks Krithika Srinivasan, a lecturer in Human Geography at the University of Edinburgh. In a column published in *The Hindu*, she then goes on to explain with remarkable clarity the reason why the well-off across the world—including, perhaps most shockingly, India—have demanded and supported stringent lockdowns:

> [C]ommunicable diseases have become strongly associated with poverty. To be then suddenly faced with a contagious disease that can kill and that cannot be avoided with better nutrition and living conditions must be deeply unsettling. Money and social privilege have temporarily lost their protective function…Perhaps this explains why COVID-19 has generated so much fear among the wealthy and the middle classes even though its impacts and death

> toll pale in comparison to diseases of the poor such as diarrhoeal disease and tuberculosis, each of which kills around 1.3 million people every year. Perhaps this explains the lack of resistance to the 'There Is No Alternative' to lockdown narrative...
>
> With COVID-19, we have become acutely aware that our health is tied to others...We want the state to take 'strong' measures that protect us from the rest of society, the rest of humanity. The poor have always known this—that their health is not within their control; that the choice is between drinking no water at all and drinking contaminated water. But their lives have not mattered enough to generate the kind of state-led action that COVID-19 has.[15]

*

Pratik Chakrabarti, Chair in History of Science and Medicine at the University of Manchester, reminds us that 'while the virus may be new, the modes of its control and prevention are not'; that state policies to control COVID-19 have a clear colonial legacy. The restrictions of the lockdown 'appear unprecedented', but in fact 'they reproduce measures that colonial governments and public health officials used [in the past] to segregate, isolate and confine people during epidemics'. During the 1896 plague in Bombay, the state 'acquired special legal and judicial powers for an apparently humanitarian cause: to prevent the spread of the epidemic'. And these enormously expanded powers of government 'specifically targeted the poor and the migrant workers [who were] seen as the carriers of the disease, restricting their movements, demolishing their homes, and subjecting their bodies to medical experiments. This became the model for subsequent governments to use disease or epidemics to justify authoritarian measures, all the way into the current pandemic.'

It is instructive that in the year 2020, a democratically elected government of free India invoked the Epidemic Diseases Act of 1897, passed by the British colonial administration during the plague epidemic, to impose its draconian lockdown restrictions.[16] This time, too, the poor and migrant workers were specifically targeted.

The lockdown did nothing to safeguard the working poor from contagion. Instead, overnight it annihilated all demand and all supply in the economy, killing or critically jeopardizing both small and large enterprises, leading to job losses of a scale never seen in recent history, and also a hiring freeze across all sectors which is likely to last a very long time. The rating agency ICRA estimates that India is set to experience an overall contraction of 9.5% in its economy due to the long and stringent lockdowns[17], which would make this the worst year for the economy since Independence. India's former chief statistician Pronab Sen fears the contraction could be even higher, at around 13%. The effect of this on jobs and livelihoods cannot be overstated. Even before the lockdown, unemployment was at a 45-year high. The gradual and fits-and-starts unlocking of the country after the lockdown of over two months did not seem to restore employment even to this low level. According to the Centre for Monitoring Indian Economy (CMIE), rural unemployment rose to 7.66% in the week ending 26 July [2020] from the 7.1% reported in the previous week. 'The national unemployment rate also inched up to 8.21% in the week ended 26 July as against 7.94% in the week to 19 July and 7.44% in the week to 12 July.'[18]

At the end of July, in one of the few official admissions of the gravity of the crisis in the economy, the union government's Micro Small and Medium Enterprises (MSME) Department predicted that almost ten crore jobs would be lost in this sector owing to the contraction of the economy.[19] However, even these high unemployment figures mask the full extent of the employment distress—in the absence of unemployment support from the state the poor cannot afford to remain without any work for even a short time, because then they would certainly starve. So most fall back on some kind of low-end self-employment or intermittent casual work which can bring in at least a dribble of money and some food for the household.

For the rich and middle-classes, the lockdown was disorienting and a nuisance, but largely seen as necessary. The consequent contraction of the economy has been painful, damaging profitability, even threatening the survival of some enterprises, and ushering in a long period of uncertainty and job losses (although, curiously, the super-rich have got richer during the pandemic[20]). But for the labouring poor who have no safety nets, the lockdown, from its very beginning, meant a sudden cataclysmic thrust into mass hunger, mass unemployment and torturous dislocations.

India's appallingly planned lockdown provided almost zero protection to the poor. Yet it placed the burden of the most destructive costs on their shoulders. That the Indian state chose a strategy which excluded the poor from its public health protections simply because these were impossible in their living conditions was an act of profound public immorality. The immorality would have been unforgivable even if the state had ensured full wage transfers to the working poor throughout the lockdown in order to cushion them from the worst effects of the loss of livelihood. As it turned out, the public immorality grew into public *criminality* because the state did not make *even partial* wage transfers. In fact, it did virtually nothing to adequately shield the already disadvantaged Indian from further insecurity and destitution.

For months, as the pandemic spread across international borders and it was clear that it would also reach India, or, more likely, already had, the government remained complacent. As late as 13 March, just eleven days before the country was locked down, officials from the Ministry of Health & Family Welfare, Government of India, declared that 'Coronavirus is not a health emergency, and that there was 'no need to panic'.[21] When it became obvious, within days, that some kind of strategy to contain infections could no longer be delayed, the state and big business quietly but decisively abandoned the poor and the vulnerable. In all the policy choices of the Indian government, it was apparent that while some lives were to be protected, others were dispensable. Journalist Ipsita Chakravarty, writing in *Scroll*, stated the terrible truth in stark, clear words: 'With the nationwide lockdown, the government drew a cordon around the bodies it wished to protect…pulling up the drawbridges to guard the chosen—those who could afford to stay in. On the bodies of those outside this charmed circle, the lockdown wrought havoc.'[22]

3

The Migrant Road: How Far Is Home?

There are many deep gashes left by the lockdown which will not heal for decades. But perhaps the deepest, which will scar the psyche of generations, is the collective wound of the several million migrant workers wilfully forsaken by their government, by their employers, and by a society whose very existence rests on their skill and labour.

Trapped without work and blockaded by an unmerciful state, these workers made perilous journeys to their villages

across India. With all vehicles without special official passes off the roads, public transport suspended and interstate transport banned, unending streams of men, women and children desperately trudged or cycled for days on burning highways. A 'fortunate' few paid to be packed into the back of trucks or airless containers, where some of them died.

Chinmay Tumbe estimates that three crore, or 30 million, interstate migrants—around 15-20% of the country's workforce—returned home between mid-March and early June. Amitabh Kundu's estimate is 22 million.[23] Both of these computations are considerably higher than the populations displaced during India's Partition, estimated at 12 to 14 million people. The Partition, in turn, is remembered as the largest forced movement of human populations in history, barring the movement of Africans trafficked as slaves to the Americas.

Through the wrenching images of these epic journeys, the migrant worker became visible to the urban middle-class as though for the first time. But the paradox is that this 'invisible' migrant worker is ubiquitous in every middle-class person's daily life. Indeed, the life that people like us live is literally built and sustained by their work. They erect our homes and offices. They bake the bricks and mine the stones that go into the walls and foundations of our homes. They plumb our pipes, fix our electricity and paint our walls. They clean our houses, bathrooms, streets and drains and climb into our sewers, sometimes drowning in them. They cook and serve our food. They tend to our children and old parents (it is this care-work that enables many in the middle class to work and enjoy the leisure of meeting friends, dining out, or catching the latest movie at the cinema). They deliver our newspapers and milk and sell us vegetables and fruit. They drive and repair our cars, taxis and school buses; they drive the auto- and e-rickshaws and pull the cycle-rickshaws without which the cities we live in—and think we own—would come to a standstill. They weave and stitch our clothes. They make and repair our shoes. They polish our gems and guard the homes and lockers in which we hoard our wealth. They work 12 to 16 hours a day in suffocating sweatshops or in the confines of their hovels to meet our needs and satisfy our luxuries.

And yet, until the brutal lockdown brought them briefly to our television and mobile phone screens—until they became tragic, dramatic news that the media could no longer ignore—we knew very little about them, and cared even less. It is telling that even estimates of their numbers vary widely. The Economic Survey of 2017 placed the number of interstate migrants at six crore. Most scholars dispute this number, but offer estimates that differ hugely—a few peg the numbers at four crore, some at ten crore, some others at fifteen crore.[24] These confusing variations reflect both official and social neglect of the massive army of labour, even though they power the economy. For a true sense of the number of human beings we have effectively banished from our consciousness, consider this: even by conservative estimates, with the families of the workers included, the numbers of migrants in India's cities and industrial townships could actually be upwards of 30 crore, or 300 million.

There is also confusion about definitions. There are in fact many kinds of migrant workers. The most disadvantaged among them are the circular migrants. They were evocatively described by renowned sociologist Jan Breman as the 'hunters and gatherers of work'. Usually landless, and of disadvantaged caste and tribe, they are desperate for any work on any terms in any corner of the country. They are often recruited by labour contractors and work against an advance as semi-bonded labour. Brick kilns and construction sites typically employ large numbers of circular migrants. They don't have fixed locations or employers, and therefore no social capital whatsoever in the host destination in which they find themselves at any point of time.

Then there are migrants who return regularly to the same destination and sometimes to the same employer, but go back to their villages one or more times a year for harvesting and festivals. These workers switch roles repeatedly from farm labour to the non-farm urban workforce in the rhythm of their hard lives.

The majority of both these categories of migrants are single men. But some also migrate circularly and seasonally with their families, such as typically the labour in brick kilns and sometimes construction sites, where entire families, very often including the children, work and live.

A third category of migrants are those with more settled employment. After a time they bring their families to the city more permanently, frequently for the dream of helping their children escape their inheritance of tough, uprooted lives through better educational opportunities. The family strikes roots in the city, however tenuous, but retains its connection with the village, returning there regularly. These relatively more settled workers form a spectrum of semi-permanent migrants, and a small number of them develop strong ties to the city, while their bonds with their villages grow weaker over time.

And finally, there are destitute people—nearly all of them

homeless—whose connections with their villages are almost completely severed, and they have nowhere to go back to.

Each of these categories of migrant workers were felled by the lockdown, and they made choices to leave or stay back and suffer based on how strong their bonds remained with their immediate or extended families in the village, and how desperate was their dispossession in the city.

Their choices were also influenced significantly by the degree to which they found support from their employers in the city. It was not only the overnight annihilation of their livelihoods that drove millions of migrants home. It was the demolition of their faith and trust—in their employers, in their middle-class neighbours, and most of all in their government. Even in normal times, they had learnt not to expect active support from the state in realizing their rights as workers and citizens. They had built their lives for the greater part *despite* the state, without even a figment of work security or wage protection, without public health care, without social housing; finding ways to carry on with their hard lives in subhuman overcrowded settlements or on the city's streets and roads. But what the pandemic and lockdown made frighteningly clear to them was that in times of crisis, their employers, the middle-classes and the government would not hesitate to simply abandon them, throw them under the bus, indifferent to their fate, leaving them to survive at best on charity food doles, and in living conditions in which the rapid spread of the virus was inevitable. They were, in the end, dispensable: an 'acceptable loss'.

The Indian state and capital—their employers—had cut them loose. And when, in their abandonment and misery, they started for their homes, the only places where they felt they would find a safe haven, the Union Home Ministry directed the state governments not to allow them to move. They were to be detained instead, and kept by force in jail-like shelter homes.

*

'We are workers, not beggars.' This was something we heard from many of the migrant workers we met. If they had to die of the Coronavirus, they said, it was better to do so among people they loved than among uncaring strangers. Besides, the way things were, they feared they would starve to death in the cities. Back in the village, there would at least be some food, they wouldn't have to beg for it.

A survey of 11,159 migrant workers by the Stranded Workers Action Network (SWAN) revealed that three weeks after the lockdown began, 50% of the migrants had rations left for less than a day, and 72% said their rations would finish in two days; 96% had not received rations from the government, and 70% had not received any cooked food from any source.[25]

A group of 240 workers in Bengaluru told SWAN, 'We are eating only one meal a day to conserve the quantum of grain we have.' Sujit Kumar, a worker from Bihar stranded in Bhatinda, Punjab, had not eaten in four days when one of our volunteers spoke with him on 3rd April. Yasmeen, a tenth-standard student in Noida, said, 'We have four babies in the house for whom we need milk; we have been feeding them sugar water these days.'

Rakesh Kumar, a migrant electrician in Bengaluru, spoke of feeling defeated and diminished because the lockdown had turned him into a beggar. He described standing in queues for food every day as 'a humiliation for a lifetime...The government did not give us anything and the food we got was from charities. Even to get that, we faced discrimination, with locals getting first preference...Being a migrant became a curse.'[26]

Twenty-two-year-old Sudhir Kumar Rajak, from Godda, Jharkhand, was in Goa when the lockdown was announced, working as a house painter. He had started working when he was 16, travelling to cities and towns across the country, wherever there was work for a decent wage. He dug sewers, lugged heavy stones—'every work the poor do, I have done'—but he also studied alongside, saving money to join college one day. Until the virus came, he liked Goa. The wages were good and regular and the people accepted outsiders. But with the pandemic, he suddenly became a pariah. He had known hardship before, but locked in the room he shared with three other migrants, for the first time he experienced the torment of depending on others for food. 'On March 25, after everything got finished, I panicked,' he told Smita Nair of *The Indian Express*. He and other workers asked local leaders in Goa for help, who told them they should get in touch with their MLAs back in Jharkhand. When they called the office of the Godda MLA, someone in his staff asked them, 'Why did you go to Goa?' Sudhir was given the number of a labour helpline, but he realised very soon that there would be no help; migrants like him were no one's responsibility:

> Earlier, I was also given a labour helpline. First they ask for some details; then they ask a new set of questions. Now they want some lists. I have decided not to waste time calling...They start their questions on the belief that we

> are hoarding food. I want them to come home and inspect our rooms. You will smell the stench of men not having taken a bath. You will see gruel stains on the floor and the last bits of salt…The other day, someone woke up in the middle of the day mumbling nonsense, [he had] no sense of time. No one reacted. He went back to sleep. We have started talking about death in normal conversations now. It's painful…The other day someone said, "Why not just step out and die of Corona, at least we will be counted somewhere."…The last pieces of money we had were spent in the initial days when vegetables were double the price, and atta Rs 50 extra. Now we eat one meal. I have not even purchased a soap as I only have some of the last bits of the Rs 500 I had left…There are 800 of us [in this *basti*], with no jobs, sitting in our rooms now…I will do everything the government tells me if they can take me to my mother.[27]

The resolve, taken by millions separately and yet in a strange unison of purpose, was to journey home, *whatever* it took. The reaction of the central and state governments was consistently callous, even cruel, blaming the migrants for not being grateful for the state's food distribution, for being misled by rumours, for being irresponsible in spreading the contagion, and for not waiting obediently for the time when the government would unlock the economy and their labour would once again be needed to engine the recovery. The state, in effect, wanted the migrants to remain invisible and obedient in their suffering to the point of death. It appeared to have no conception of them as equal citizens of the republic, and it seemed shorn even of elementary compassion.

With the first wave of movement that began in late March, governments sealed borders between states, beat and arrested the migrants travelling on foot, and confined them to crowded, sub-human quarantine centres. (The trapped migrants called these centres jails—'*qaid*', or prison, and '*qaidee*', or prisoner', were the words they used.[28]) Hundreds of thousands still persisted, walking through village pathways, away from the highways being patrolled by the police; or hiding in claustrophobic truck containers and, at least in one case, inside a cement mixer. Many ate just biscuits and slept on the hard road or railway tracks.

The price of seats on the few buses that had special passes to run or just a little space in the back of a truck sky-rocketed. There was rampant profiteering, as truck and bus drivers explained that they had to pay bribes to the police all along the highway. One group of returning migrants told me that they paid 2000 rupees for space on the roof of a crowded bus. It was twice this cost inside the bus. In these private buses and trucks passengers were packed in ways that made the spread of the contagion very likely.

Few could afford these rates—and in any case, even these private buses and trucks that could run on the highways due

to some tenuous exemption they had negotiated or because bribes had been paid, were rare. So most people walked. Some spent their last savings, or asked their impoverished families back in the villages to wire them money, so that they could buy a bicycle.

Among the millions who trudged home were Sakka Bhuria and her husband, both daily wage labourers in Ahmedabad, and their seven-year-old son. They walked and hitched rides to their village in Jhabua district of Madhya Pradesh, 300 kilometres away, with just some biscuits and a can of water to sustain themselves. At one point, they had to wade across a river. Safeena Khatun walked with her husband over a thousand kilometres from the brick kiln in Jharkhand's Madhopur, where they worked, to their home in Uttar Pradesh's Moradabad district. They took turns sleeping on the road, with the husband staying up at night to keep guard. They did not know what they would do in the village—'We have family in our village, nothing else,' said Safeena—but at least they wouldn't starve.[29] Nikita, seven months pregnant, walked with a group of 20 from Ghansoli in Navi Mumbai to her village in Buldhana, Maharashtra, a journey of over 480 kilometres, sitting down 'once in a while' when she was exhausted.[30] Kajodi, 90 years old, made her 100-kilometre journey leaning on a long stick and pushing herself forward step by step. Her family sold toys at traffic lights in one of Delhi's suburbs. Now they had no option but to walk back to their village in Rajasthan. With just a few packets of biscuits between them, they smoked handmade beedis to kill their hunger.[31]

The migrants encountered unexpected kindness but also cruelty along the way. Sukhdev Singh, his pregnant wife and six-year-old daughter, and a score of other families, trekked for nine days from Jaisalmer in Rajasthan to their village in Punjab. They would travel each year from Muktar in Punjab to Jaisalmer to harvest the green gram crop. But this trek was different. Beaten back by the police, repelled by villagers, they were forced to walk through deserts and wilderness. 'No one helped us on the way, no one allowed us even to drink water from irrigation channels. If villagers saw us, they clearly told us [to go], we may infect their water…We were not allowed to enter any village along the way even if we only wanted to rest under shade of a tree.'[32]

Seventeen-year-old Baliram Kumar made it to UP's Gorakhpur district from Bengaluru after walking for 25 days. He was with a group of 15 who became nocturnal creatures in order to survive the heat and the police. 'We walked from 3 a.m. to 10 a.m. and rested during the day,' he told *Scroll*. 'My feet are cut and scabbed…I had shoes but what good are shoes after a while? I'm so tired. My whole body is aching.' Twenty-year-old Vinod Yadav made an even longer journey, also from Bengaluru, with another group, walking for 27 days to reach Bihar's Katihar district. 'I got a fever two or three times,' he said. 'I would buy medicines from the villages we were passing through and keep going. Sometimes we rested in the villages for a day or two.' Their only shelter was the shade of trees. For food, they had carried sattu, a mix of ground pulses and cereals which did not need cooking, just some water and salt.[33]

Stories emerged of the rarest human endurance, such as that of 15-year-old Jyoti Kumari who cycled 1200 kilometres on a second-hand bicycle, with her injured father travelling pillion, from Delhi to Darbhanga in Bihar. And 11-year-old

Tabaraak, who rode a tricycle cart carrying his blind mother and injured father from Varanasi to Araria, a distance of 600 kilometres. These epic feats were celebrated widely, but these should in fact have been occasions for collective introspection and national shame—that our children were driven to these dangerous limits of physical and psychological endurance by a government that refused to care.

Several migrants died of exhaustion on the way. Jamlo Madkam, a 12-year-old Adivasi girl from a village in the Bijapur district of Chhattisgarh, worked in the chilli fields of Telangana. On 15 April, she started walking back to Bijapur with 11 other labourers, some of them children like her. They took a forest route because the main road was closed. They had covered over 100 kilometres by the morning of the third day when Jamlo complained of stomach pain and headache. She died shortly after, just about an hour's walk from her village. Jamlo's parents barely make a living by collecting forest produce. When journalist Kamlesh Painkra met them, Jamlo's mother said to him, 'I gave birth to eight children, and of them four died at the age of crawling. Now Jamlo is dead too.' The chief medical officer of Bijapur district told journalists, 'She might have collapsed due to exhaustion and muscle fatigue, which may not figure in the post mortem report. She also fell down on the way and was injured the previous day, say the other labourers...When I sent an ambulance [around 11 a.m.] they had already walked about 5-6 kilometres with the dead body.'[34]

Two young friends, Amrit Kumar and Mohammad Saiyub, were returning from Surat in Gujarat, where both worked 16-hour shifts in a textile unit, to their village Devari in Basti, Uttar Pradesh. It was the middle of May, with day temperatures well over 40 degrees Celsius, and they were travelling in the back of a truck with 50 to 60 other men. They were passing through Madhya Pradesh when Amrit developed a fever. His co-travellers feared he had COVID and offloaded him, but Saiyub would not abandon his friend and got off the truck to be with him. Amrit collapsed by the side of the road and Saiyub held him in his lap, trying to revive him, shielding him from the sun and cupping water to his parched lips. When a politician arrived to distribute food to migrants walking on the highway, Saiyub begged him to call an ambulance. Amrit died of heatstroke two days later in a hospital in Shivpuri. It was another two days before Saiyub could take his friend back to Devari. Officials in Basti had made it clear to their counterparts in Shivpuri that they would not allow the body into their district unless a test confirmed that Amrit had not died of COVID.[35]

Hemlata Singh would have felt luckier than most as she set out with her husband Nihal Singh for their village in Morena, Madhya Pradesh. Nihal Singh drove an auto-rickshaw in Ahmedabad. After the lockdown, he recalled, 'I was sitting at home for a month and a half. We had no money left to eat, our landlord was asking us for rent. It was better to die in our village than starve to death in the city. If I died alone in the city, my parents would worry.' He resolved to take his wife and two children, his two brothers and their families, to Morena in his auto-rickshaw. It would be a 1200-kilometre drive, but Nihal was confident about driving the distance. And then near Shivpuri a truck hit them, injuring Hemlata most of all. The local government hospital tested and found her negative for COVID, but refused to treat her for anything else and let her die.

Turned away at the Gujarat-Rajasthan border, four migrant workers walking to their village in Rajasthan were mowed down by a truck on a dark highway. Sixteen migrant workers, exhausted walking from Jalna in Maharashtra to Shahdol in Madhya Pradesh, slept on a railway track, which they believed would be safe since no trains were running. No one had told them that only passenger services had been suspended. They were run over by a goods train.

According to one estimate, by the beginning of June, more than 200 people had died on the roads travelling home, due to exhaustion, hunger, heat-stroke and accidents.[36]

Two doctors explained to *Scroll* what toll the days and weeks of walking would have taken on the human body. Dr Yogesh Jain, who works with tribal and rural communities in Chhattisgarh, said it takes 60 to 70 calories to be able to walk a single kilometre. A large meal provides 600 calories, which one would consume walking 8 to 10 kilometres. 'And these are calculations that have been done in 25 degrees [Celsius] temperature, when you are not undernourished, lifting weights or stressed.' But migrants walked over 20 or 30 kilometres a day, often with no food and in temperatures close to 40 degrees. As one keeps walking, Yogesh Jain explained, the mechanisms in our bodies to produce energy slow down. The production of glucose, the final substance that is metabolised to release energy, falls in tired bodies. 'If your blood glucose falls short and there is not enough glucose to run your system, it would cause you to feel drowsy, pass out and die of starvation.' In addition to this, in the hot sun, there is dehydration, or water loss, causing electrolyte imbalance and driving down sodium levels, which can result in heat-strokes.[37]

The extreme endurance that the migrants displayed is a monumental tragedy. It is not a choice they made. They did not march or pedal hundreds of kilometres with little sustenance in order to earn our amazement and admiration, or rewards from sports federations (the Cycling Federation of India, for instance, was 'impressed' by Jyoti Kumari's 'pedalling capacity' and decided to 'give her a chance to prove her mettle'[38]). What the migrant workers and their families endured was yet another, perhaps the most painful, chapter in the story of their lives scripted by a profoundly callous state and an unjust, unequal society.

According to a doctor quoted in *Scroll*, 'to talk about the march as exceptional [is] to forget the way systemic negligence [has] routinely ravaged the bodies of the poor'. Dr Gargi Goyel, who practices in Rajasthan's Udaipur district, further pointed out that the migrant workers walked with quiet confidence born from a lifetime of suffering: The bodies of workers are moulded by the back-breaking work they do on farms, factories and construction sites. 'They're brave—they know their body can do it,' Dr Goyel said. 'They don't want to wait for the government because the government has done nothing for them...They are already malnourished. Already their bodies are trained to deal with minimal food and do strenuous activity.' [39]

The central and state governments offered no relief of any kind to the workers on the road. In fact, they did the opposite. When some senior IAS officers in Delhi organized buses for migrants who wanted to return, they were reprimanded, suspended and removed from their postings.[40] Many migrant workers reported being beaten like fugitives from the law by the police. In mid-May, more than 500 migrant labourers from Bihar, Jharkhand, Odisha and other states were assaulted by police in Vijayawada. They were returning from establishments that had shut down in Tamil Nadu and Andhra Pradesh when they were stopped on the highway by the Andhra police and told to go back. When the workers refused, the police resorted to a vicious lathi charge. 'We will never return to AP again. Hundreds of workers are walking on the roads for more than a month and the officials did not even offer us a packet of biscuits. Instead of helping the poor, the police are beating us mercilessly,' a woman labourer said.[41]

Twenty-five-year-old Kundan cycled 1,100 kilometres to reach Patna from Panipat. He survived not only exhaustion and hunger but also intimidation and violence. After three days on the road, he was stopped on an expressway by the police. 'You have money for cycles and not for food?' they said as they beat him.[42] Salman Ravi, a journalist with BBC Hindi found a group of labourers in Delhi who had been beaten by the police when they stopped by a road to eat the food they were carrying. They had been walking and cycling from Ambala for six days already, returning to their villages in Madhya Pradesh. One man with two little children and the family's bedding on an old bicycle broke down as he spoke of what had been done to them.

> 'What Modi ji has done is good, he has been very good to us. If we're hungry we'll find something, we'll manage. But at least he's comfortable where he is...Arrey, shouldn't he think of people who are poor? They are in distress, shouldn't he do something? But never mind about us, we'll go away, we'll die, we'll take our children and we'll leave somehow...We're in great difficulty, sir, we're helpless,

> look at our kids....[The police] chased us away from that border, now they'll drive us away from here. So where do we go now? We're coming from Ambala, it's been six days...We bought someone's broken-down cycle for 500 rupees, this is how we've been travelling...But everything is all right, all is well—those people, they're fine where they are, they're getting food to eat, aren't they? They make a phone call and get what they want. Who cares about us?...We come here and the police thrash us with sticks. They beat a man there so badly he collapsed on the road. Is this how things should be?'[43]

Utterly broken by the suffering and indignity, a particularly anguished migrant labourer from Jharkhand working in Mumbai said. '*Modi ki nazron mein hum keede hi hain na, waisi hi maut marenge.*' (We are mere insects in Modi's eyes, so that is how we'll die.)[44]

Worker families who ultimately reached their destinations were sometimes rounded up and made to squat on the road and hosed down with unsafe disinfectants as though they were vermin. Villagers were frequently unwelcoming, and forced the migrants into poorly maintained quarantine centres outside the village borders. Many built blockades, refusing to allow any outsider to walk through their villages.

State borders became like international borders of hostile fiefdoms. The Maharashtra government transported workers to the borders of neighbouring Madhya Pradesh. Here they were blocked for several days by the MP police, without food or water, and beaten when they protested. Lockdown and transport rules were announced abruptly and were poorly communicated, and changed whimsically and abruptly. For instance, there was confusion among many migrant workers regarding whether to register with the home or the host state in order to return to their homes via government-arranged Shramik trains. A worker from Jharkhand in Sindhudurg, Maharashtra told *Scroll:* 'On WhatsApp I got a message saying we have to register on the Jharkhand government website if we want to go home to Jharkhand, so I have done that. I have not heard anything about registering with the Maharashtra police too. I have no money to pay for anything, so I have left everything in the hands of the Jharkhand government.'[45] The Maharashtra government guidelines allowed any doctor to issue a medical certificate, which was mandatory for a migrant to be allowed to travel outside the state. But when Shivam Rathod from Bihar, a construction worker in Mumbai, reported to the police for permission to travel, he was told that his medical clearance certificate could not be signed by just any doctor, he must go to a government hospital to seek the medical clearance.

My colleagues and I spoke to several migrants one night at the Delhi-UP border at Gazipur. We had rushed there responding to scores of distress calls. Large numbers of migrants were gathered there, pushed back by the police.

The Uttar Pradesh government had suddenly decided that it would not allow them to walk across the border. Those who could afford to hire taxis could, inexplicably, cross. Others, many of them women and children, had to spend several nights sleeping at the border, subsisting on food brought in by kindly locals and hoping the government would change its mind.

The situation was even worse in other regions. At the UP-Madhya Pradesh border, huge numbers were stranded for days, with neither state wanting them in its territory. In early May, Kumar Abhishek of *India Today* reported: 'Thousands of migrant labourers from Gujarat and Maharashtra reached Kaimaha village in Mahoba district in hundreds of buses. However, the district administration has not allowed them to enter further into the state. These migrant workers, hungry, thirsty and shelterless, are braving the scorching heat. Pregnant women and children are sleeping under vehicles to get some relief from the unbearable heat...Neither is the Mahoba district administration allowing the migrant workers to cross into [UP], nor is the Madhya Pradesh government taking them back...these people have nowhere else to go[.]'[46]

In stark contrast, 300 special buses were sent by the UP government to bring back students stranded in Rajasthan's Kota town, a hub of coaching centres for competitive exams to engineering and medical colleges that middle-class students aspire to. The air-conditioned buses were stocked with food, mineral water bottles, sanitizers and masks.[47] Other states like Maharashtra, Uttarakhand, Assam, Chhattisgarh and Punjab followed the UP example. For Indians stranded abroad because of lockdowns in those countries, the Government of India initiated its much-vaunted 'Vande Bharat Mission'. Under this emotive 'nationalist' banner, the union government deployed its national carrier, Air India, to bring expatriate Indians home at pre-fixed fares. Eventually, almost ten lakh Indians returned home through this programme.

The Indian state seemed not in the least ashamed or embarrassed about this open display of class bias in its treatment of impoverished internal migrants on the one hand, and middle-class students and Indians working abroad, on the other. This class bias became the hallmark of every policy choice of the union government in its response to the COVID-19 pandemic.

Studies now show that forcing migrants to stay in the cities at the start of the lockdown actually worsened the spread of the Coronavirus to rural India. Two community-service doctors in rural Rajasthan, Pavitra Mohan and Arpita Amin, observe correctly that there were actually two waves of the movement of migrants. The first started in late March and continued until mid-April. Strict and often brutal policing, locking large numbers in quarantine centres, and some food support by NGOs and many city administrations halted this movement. The second phase began on 4th May, when the government of India finally allowed interstate movement through special trains and buses.[48] Mohan and Amin used public data to plot the numbers of confirmed COVID-19 cases in Rajasthan. Until April 7, the numbers of median COVID-19 cases increased only marginally from zero to 1.5 per district, despite massive numbers of returning migrants. But between May 4 and May 15, the median numbers of cases per district increased from 1.5 to 30. This is further proof that the decision of the government to block migrant travel was an act of criminal public cruelty. Mohan and Amin conclude that 'most migrants who returned soon after lockdown had much lower risk of being infected and did not contribute to any significant spread subsequently. Held back in cities when the epidemic was raging there, the migrants picked up the infection. When they finally returned from May 4, the epidemic spread to rural areas. Allowing the migrants to return before the lockdown would have contained the epidemic in the cities, in addition to saving so much misery and violation of human rights that will continue to haunt all Indian citizens for decades to come'.[49]

*

Postscript

In the midst of spectacular state cruelty, there were individual gestures of empathy. A touching story is told of a migrant worker who was stranded with his disabled son in Bharatpur, Rajasthan. Desperate to return to his home in Bareilly, Uttar Pradesh, a journey of 250 kilometres, he stole a bicycle from outside the home of one Sahab Singh. Sweeping his verandah the next morning, Singh found a letter of apology. '*Main aapki cycle lekar jaa raha hoon. Ho sake toh mujhe maaf kar dena ji, kyunki mere paas koi saadhan nahi tha. Mera ek bachcha hai uske liye aisa karna pada kyunki woh viklang hai, chal nahi sakta. Humein Bareilly tak jaana hai.*' (I'm taking your bicycle. Please forgive me if you can, because I had no other means. I had to do it for the sake of my child who is handicapped, he cannot walk. We have to go to Bareilly.) The letter was signed '*Aap ka kusoorwar, ek yatri, majboor ek mazdoor, Mohammed Iqbal Khan*'—'Your culprit, a traveller, a helpless labourer, Mohammed Iqbal Khan.'

Singh, probably not much better off than Khan, decided not to file a complaint with the police.

4

Wayward Trains

It was only after five weeks of lockdown and searing images of thousands of walking migrants, many with small children, appearing daily on the front pages of newspapers and on television screens around the world, that the union government announced a series of special Shramik or 'Worker' trains. This raised hope for some belated display of humanity by state authorities, and an acceptance in principle of both the right of migrants to return to their villages, and the state's responsibility to support them to safely travel home.

But these hopes were short-lived. For one, the state ran too few trains for the numbers who needed them, and then enmeshed the workers in complex and opaque on-line bureaucratic processes—requiring them initially to pay for their travel—and ran the trains without food and water for long stretches.

To get a seat on the Shramik trains, migrants were required to register and get clearances from their home states, agreement from the host states where they were working, and medical certificates attesting that they were COVID free. It was very difficult for migrants, more so in a city which was not their home, to get a doctor to sign a certificate of good health. Remember, this was during the period of total lockdown, during which even a middle-class person would have been hard-pressed to venture outside her home and find and persuade a doctor to certify that she was COVID-free. This was mandatory even for bus travel. This also cost money. A mason from Jharkhand in Mumbai's Dharavi slum said he had been reduced to eating just one meal given by a charity. He gave all his savings to someone who said he would organize a bus to Jharkhand, and disappeared. When trains were started, social workers helped him fill the registration form, but he hit a road-block because he could not organize a health certificate. A local activist told *Scroll* that they did organize medical check-ups for the workers, but she was worried that many migrant workers might be classified as symptomatic for COVID-19 even if they were not infected. This would not only block their chances of returning but also endanger their health, as they would be locked up in insanitary quarantine centres. 'These labourers live and work next to a landfill, in the most squalid conditions, so they are often sick with cough, cold, fever and breathing problems,' the activist said. 'They may not have COVID, but if they don't pass the medical test, will they be allowed to go home?[50]

For most migrants, getting a seat on one of these special trains was like winning a jackpot in a whimsical lottery. Not only were the on-line registration procedures convoluted and required smart-phones, literacy and technical skills that they did not always possess, their chances were also 'completely dependent on destination states that either approve[d] or put on hold district-based lists with no clear explanation'.[51] By contrast, those who could afford air-conditioned Rajdhani trains just had to buy a ticket and travel.[52] No official, again, seemed perturbed by the obvious class bias in these different rules.

The rules were also, once more, confusing. Many workers were told that those wanting to travel had to apply at the local police station. They did that, and were then told that they had to apply on-line to their respective state governments. Some found educated workers who helped them do this. But even after many days they were not allotted a seat on any train. A worker in Mumbai, Rathod, seethed, 'I feel so angry at the way they are treating us, but I can't even express my anger in public. If we want to go home, we have to stay quiet.'[53]

Despite all these barriers, masses of migrants, unable to afford the rent for their rooms and with no savings left for food, gathered in large crowds outside railway stations. Many had to wait for several days before they found a seat. Many more did not, and set out finally on foot.

Vibha Devi, eight months pregnant, lived with her husband, a construction worker, and two children in Faridabad near Delhi. Her husband's employer neither paid him nor answered his calls. The 500 rupees that Vibha had received in April in her Jan Dhan account as part of the union government's lockdown relief package hadn't lasted long (there is no zero missing, that really is the figure: a paltry Rs 500). The family survived in the city for 50 days after the lockdown was announced mainly because Vibha Devi's mother wired them her pension savings of Rs 1500 from her village in Samastipur, Bihar. They still had to rely often on food charity. When it became impossible to sustain themselves, they decided to return to Bihar. They walked for two days to New Delhi Railway Station after the Shramik trains were announced. They walked because no one in the government and bureaucracy had thought about how people would reach railway stations when there was no intra-city public transport of any kind allowed. And then for four days, they waited outside the railway station, fighting hunger and dodging the police, and sleeping on the pavement, but no train arrived. No one told them no Shramik trains operated from New Delhi Railway station. Finally, they reached Anand Vihar station, were checked for fever, and at last boarded a train to Bihar. But even this did not mark a happy ending for them. Their fellow-villagers did not welcome them back, suspecting them of carrying the virus, although they kept showing certificates from doctors that they were not infected.[54]

Despite the fact that they had been locked down, without work and wages, for several weeks, the union government initially required workers to pay for their tickets—the cost of a sleeper berth, with a top-up for 'super-fast' travel! It was only after nation-wide outrage (and a rare political gesture by the Congress party of shaming the government by offering to pay for the tickets) that the government back-tracked. It also turned out that the price of tickets on many of the special migrant trains was in fact higher than what it would have been for normal train tickets.[55] The union government also claimed that it was in any case giving an 85% subsidy on the Shramik train fare from day one, but when a PIL on the problems being faced by migrant workers came up in the Supreme Court, the government admitted that this was not the case. The cost of the tickets was being borne by the state governments.[56]

In response to a Right to Information application by the

Wire Hindi, the Railway Department revealed that it collected 4.80 crore rupees from migrant workers in May and 2.11 crore rupees in June (in violation of the orders of the Supreme Court which by then had instructed the government not to charge workers for their travel).[57] For any government this is an utterly trivial amount. It could also have most easily been borne from the donations of several thousand crore rupees to the completely opaque and gratuitous PM CARES fund set up by the Modi administration. But the government chose to extract this amount from dispossessed workers whom it had made jobless and brought to the brink of starvation.

The union government then seemed to have second thoughts about facilitating the travel of migrants altogether, with the union home secretary issuing a directive that interstate travel would be allowed only for 'distressed' persons, and not for those 'residing normally at places other than native places for purposes of work'.[58] This in effect ruled out the return of migrants. Again, after widespread outrage, this directive was not acted upon, although I don't think it was officially withdrawn.

The chief minister of Karnataka cancelled all worker trains following a meeting with leading builders, who complained that they would not be able to kickstart construction work if the migrants were allowed to leave.[59] I do not have accounts of what the chief minister said to them. I doubt he reminded them that the workers would not have felt compelled to leave if they had been paid wages for the period of the lockdown. Once again, after public criticism, he withdrew his ban and the trains started to run again out of Karnataka after a few days.

Those who were fortunate enough to get a seat on a train

had further ordeals to endure. On many trains there was no food or water for hours, the toilets were unusable because there was no water in the taps or flushes, and inexplicably the trains would lose their way and arrive at their destination many hours and sometimes days late. A particularly notorious example was of a train from Mumbai to Gorakhpur in Uttar Pradesh: the travellers were astounded to find themselves instead in faraway Rourkela in Odisha!

The Railway Protection Force reported that at least 80 people died of dehydration or hunger on these train journeys.[60] It took four days to discover the body of a 37-year-old driver from Mumbai who died in the toilet of one of these trains, which meant that these had not been cleaned even after several days of travel. Nandita Haksar describes a harrowing journey of migrant workers from the North-East from Goa to Manipur, which should have taken 64 hours but took 119, and for the most part there was no food and water for the passengers, and no water in the toilets.[61]

It took the shattering image of a lifeless young woman, who had collapsed and died at the Muzaffarpur railway station, probably from extreme dehydration and food deprivation while travelling from Ahmedabad, and her baby son trying to awaken her, to finally stir the conscience of the nation. But there were still no apologies and little changed for the better.

5

Fragile Refuge

Twenty-two-year-old Satvir, a migrant on one of the buses that Karwan-e-Mohabbat managed to organize, said to us firmly, 'Whatever happens, I'm not coming back to Delhi. Look at my two small children. We had been reduced to charity for food. For days we were not allowed to cross the Delhi border. We will eat less, we will manage with whatever we get. But I will not make my children go through such suffering again.'

Twenty-year-old Vivek Mishra worked at a restaurant in Karol Bagh. The lockdown had broken him. 'Seeing how badly we were treated, just abandoned when we needed the city most…I'm never going back,' he said, speaking to the *Indian Express* from his village home in UP's Gonda district. The residents of his village hadn't been welcoming, denying him entry till he had quarantined himself for 15 days in a vacant shop. But this was still home. 'We are farmers, we can sustain ourselves,' he said.[62]

Penniless and fearing starvation after 40 days of the lockdown, 45-year-old Lokanath Swain, a power-loom worker in Surat, was finally able to take a train to his village in Odisha's Ganjam district only after his family sent him some money. Surat has the highest migrants to locals ratio in India, at 58% of the city's population and 70% of its total waged workforce, according to a study by the migrant rights organization Aajeevika Bureau. Swain spoke to the Thomson Reuters Foundation from a quarantine centre in Odisha of his disillusionment and his firm resolve never to return to Surat: 'Nobody was understanding our problems there. My employer did not pick up his phone when I contacted him to ask for my ten days' wages pending with him. They are big people. What can we do?…I thought I would not live until the time trains would resume. How long can a starving man survive? Maybe one or two days…What is the point of returning now? My employer abandoned me. I would rather stay with my family even if I earn half of what I earned there.'

Alpa Shah and Jens Lerche of the London School of Economics explain that the business model of many modern enterprises rests on the migrant labour-force because it is 'paid less, works longer and harder, and is more flexible than local labour'. The economies of many countries depend on such a precarious migrant workforce, but mostly these workers come from other, usually poorer countries. India is a country of continental scale, and here it is internal migrants who play this role of informal contract work, and are treated as second-class citizens, without unions, often without formal contracts, 'easily controlled, cheap and dispensable'. Many—about ten crore—travel between their rural homes and faraway work sites for a part of each year. They often come from the poorest states, and most of them belong to India's historically disadvantaged minorities, Dalits and Adivasis.

Shah and Lerche also observe, importantly, that these

seasonal migrant workers are, in turn, supported by a further invisible economy—the household. Seasonal migrants can work because of 'all the work undertaken across generations at home, including care provided by the spouse, children, siblings and elderly parents'. This labour of kin 'care for the migrant workers in the seasons when there is no work, who will maintain the migrants' home so they have a place to return to, and who will care for them when employers have overworked their bodies so they are no longer fit to work'.[63] It is to this economy of care that the migrants returned when the Indian state and capital threw them to the wolves.

But the care economy of the household—the final refuge—is fragile: how long will it be able to sustain them?

Those who reached home after epic journeys were forced within weeks to begin evaluating their options. In a small survey of 132 migrant workers who had returned home, the Workers' Charter, a collective of organizations and researchers working with informal labour, found that 30% of the workers had decided not to return to the cities even after things returned to normal. For many of the remaining 70%, the decision of returning was contingent on the pandemic being controlled.[64]

Shamim, a thirtry-year-old *pheriwala*, a travelling cloth vendor, walked to his village in UP's Shamli district from Jhalod in Gujarat. It was an unimaginably hard trek of almost 900 kilometres that took him more than ten days. The nightmare seemed to be over when he was back with his family. But soon he was faced with a new challenge: he did not know how to feed his family. His wife had procured 25 kilos of wheat from the village ration shop some days before he returned, but this was quickly exhausted. When he spoke with me on the phone, a week after his return home, he said their food stocks would last them only three or four days. They had no savings and Shamim's contractor had vanished with all his earnings. They owned no land, and had received no government assistance. They could not turn to anyone in the village as everyone was struggling for survival. 'The nightmare for migrant workers will continue because the factors that made them leave villages to find employment outside have only worsened,' says Tapan Sen, general secretary of Centre of Indian Trade Unions.[65]

The exodus out of our impoverished villages will begin again. The poor have few choices.

Imteyaz Alam, a 37-year-old, worked as an electrician in Mumbai for most of his adult life. After 50 harrowing days of lockdown he was back home in UP after he managed a seat on a Shramik train. 'I am praying to Allah to find work here,' he said to Roli Srivastava and Anuradha Nagaraj, correspondents with Thomson Reuters Foundation. 'My heart does not feel like returning. If I have to die, I would rather be with my family.' Then he added, 'But if I see my family starving, I will have to forget the hardships.'[66]

Dipankar Ghose, a journalist with *The Indian Express*, spent a month, over May and June 2020, with migrants who had returned to their villages in the Bhagalpur district of Bihar. In a poignant report, he notes that hunger had driven them back to the village, but the same hunger had begun to push them back to the city. Through the trauma of sudden joblessness in the harsh city, and deprivation and hunger on special trains or in the back of trucks, memories of 'their green fields, mango trees and families' had kept them going, writes Dipankar. But 'now that they are here, that dream is falling apart, infected by reality. Bihar's villages have no work, no sustenance. It was why they left. And it is why, despite the yearning to be home at a time of crisis, they will have to leave again.'

Anil Singh earned Rs 600 a day as a mason in Delhi. His eyes welled up as he spoke to Dipankar. About a month earlier, he had paid Rs 3,500 'to be one of 70 people squashed in the back of a truck for three nights and two days [to reach his village]. He ate one packet of biscuits and six bananas over that time. But now? "*Chori karenge* (We will steal)," he says, half in jest, half in pain.'

Many of the returning migrants had been told they would be given jobs under MNREGA and other schemes and their names had been registered at the railway stations and quarantine centres, but they had got nothing. Not even the Rs 1000 they had been promised under the state government's Corona Sahayata (Corona assistance). 'The family offers comfort, and the fields some food,' writes Dipankar. 'Yet, without money, they have had to reduce purchases even of soap bars, salt, vegetables and fruit.' There was also the weight of debt. One of the migrant men, Diwakar Kumar, had taken an advance of Rs 50,000 on his salary. Others had taken Rs 4,000 to Rs 5,000 from their employers. When this ran out, what would they do if there was a medical problem, or any other need that could not be put aside? In the village, they would have to depend on the mahajans, money lenders, who lend at an interest of five per cent per month. 'Nobody survives that,' the men told Dipankar.

Twenty-one-year-old Ranjit fixed billboards in Ranchi. There was no income after the lockdown. When he left the city for his village on his motorcycle, he was beaten by the police several times. Yet he told Dipankar, 'I will leave soon...The company owes me Rs 15,000 and I'm afraid I will lose that money...All I want is to stay home and work here. But I can't. Every day I tell myself, I will leave tomorrow.'[67]

But even this is not an option for many migrants, mostly the self-employed, whose livelihoods were destroyed by the lockdown. A large number stay on in their villages unable to overcome the trauma of the lockdown, or because they have no option—with the economy in a shambles and their small savings exhausted, they will be unable to rebuild their lives for years, if ever. In October, writer Natasha Badhwar visited her father-in-law in his ancestral village in Uttar Pradesh. She found that the private school there had closed and teachers' salaries had been stopped as parents could not pay the fees or afford mobile phones for online classes. She met Azeemul, a migrant who had returned from Mumbai just after the lockdown. 'In Mumbai I live in a small kholi and sell handkerchiefs on the footpath in the town area. It's a decent life,' he told her. 'Sometimes, I go to the sea beach and feel free of all pain and worries...[But] I don't know if I will go back. I fear the police and the state. The pandemic has disrupted everything.'

Wasim, a neighbour of Natasha's family in the village, drove an Uber taxi in Delhi before the lockdown hit him. 'Unable to sustain his survival in the city, pay EMIs due on his car or send money home, Wasim has lived through a nightmare that refuses to end,' writes Natasha. 'The finance company's representatives came to his home in the village to intimidate his wife [Shagufta] for recovery of the loan. Shagufta has begun to spin thread for blankets to earn a basic sustenance.'[68]

*

It is important to remember that the most powerless among the migrants, such as adolescent girls in mills and garment factories, remained trapped despite the Shramik trains and the easing of lockdown restrictions. Nineteen-year-old Jasoda Debbarma had travelled to Tamil Nadu from Tripura with 50 other girls to work in a garment workshop near Tirupur. They were made to put in over 12 hours a day, with only a short lunch break, and lived in closely monitored hostels. Jasoda and her friends had not been paid since February and the endless back-breaking work was taking a heavy toll on them. Desperate to return to their villages, she and the other girls applied for seats on Shramik trains, and even got messages on their phones confirming they could travel. But their employers did not allow them. They had been fed during the lockdown, and now that production could recommence, they would have to get back to work. 'They [the management] called us up and started abusing us,' Jasoda told Ipsita Chakravarty of *Scroll*, 'so we started going to work again…I keep saying I want to go home until tears come to my eyes.'[69]

And then there were the most vulnerable among the wretched of the city—the homeless, who had nowhere to go, no village, no family to return to. On a summer afternoon in Delhi during the third phase of the lockdown I met a group of around 15 homeless men of different ages living in a depression on the banks of the river Yamuna, a spot strategically chosen by the men because it was hidden from view from the main road, hidden from the eyes of the police. In my work with homeless people over two decades, I have come to know the men of Yamuna Pushta more closely. I have learnt that the large majority of them are alone in the world. They have, for one reason or the other, broken all bonds with their families. With some it is the shame of not being able to provide for their families, with others it is alcoholic and abusive fathers; some are addicted to drugs and alcohol, some were born to the streets or abandoned on them. When I met the men that afternoon, they were living inside Hume pipes and under trees. The pipes, in which they had to bend double to enter, contained their only belongings, maybe one change of clothes, a gamcha, a bucket, and some vessels to cook and eat in. Through the lockdown, every single day, food was an enormous challenge for these men. Hunger was common. They had no savings, and employment was of course out of the question. They were content even in this intense hardship, because at least the police would not spot them. They still felt safe in their harsh haven, but only because they were unseen by the state. They had become, for all purposes, fugitives from the law, runaways from the terrible quarantine centres in which most homeless men had been incarcerated.

*

Back in Bihar, by July migrants had started receiving urgent calls from contractors to return to the cities. In many cases, the same employers who had cut them loose during the lockdown were now offering them flight tickets to return. With his customary empathy, reporter Dipankar Ghose spent a morning at the Patna airport, speaking with some of these migrants returning to the cities that had betrayed them. 'They stand close to each other,' he observes, 'bags slung over shoulders, noses pressed against the glass. They watch flights land and take off, passengers in PPEs being ferried in buses.' He writes of a sympathetic airport staffer, 'tasked with maintaining social distance', who speaks to the migrants gently. 'Bhai,' he asks them, 'Are you going for work? Is the situation bad at home?' And he confides, to reassure them: 'I haven't been inside an aircraft, either.'

Manish Kumar tells Dipankar he spent four days in May on a train from Delhi. Now, he will spend two hours on a plane back. He does not even know the name of the real estate company in Manesar, Haryana, which paid for his ticket. A contractor had called him, he has been assured payment of 300 rupees a day. He will have to live on-site. 'This usually means mats on the floor, and at the most, a fan and a bulb where we sleep. We know that even payments will not be on time, and not until the work is over.' He is ready for long hours of backbreaking work, perhaps one meal a day at night. 'I don't want to go,' he says. 'But the children are hungry at home.'

Another construction worker, Lal, dodged the police and his landlord in Gurgaon in March after work stopped and no one paid him wages; he survived because an NGO gave him a food packet. He said he was afraid, thinking about his wife, two daughters, and his old mother at home. 'I spent days trying to find a way home and finally left on a truck to see them. But now, I am returning to save them. There are no jobs in Bihar. Even in the village, there are expenses. How long will my children eat PDS rice and salt? How will they buy vegetables? The monsoons are here and we will need a new roof. How will we buy fertiliser and seeds? The city has COVID, I know, and the village doesn't. But no father wants his children to go hungry.'[70]

6

The Neglect of Food Security and the Dismantling of Informal Labour Rights

Just months into the pandemic, India's labouring poor disappeared from television screens and even the inner pages of newspapers. It was as though after the country had gradually unlocked and most migrants had returned home, the immense suffering of the poor, the mass hunger and destruction of work that racked their lives, had swiftly passed and left not a trace behind. It had not; it will not for years. But as a nation we have perfected the art of looking away.

I have spoken of Yamuna Pushta, on the banks of the Yamuna river, which is usually home to over 4000 homeless men. They survived by casual wage work, mostly in wedding parties or roadside eateries, or as head-loaders. Work was uncertain and always underpaid, but even on their worst days they managed to keep hunger at bay, often because of religious food charities in gurudwaras, temples and dargahs. I met them after the country formally began unlocking, and found their destitution and desperation as stark as it had been during the lockdown. There was still no work, and shrines had still not adequately revived their food charities. The Delhi government had also mostly ended its free cooked food distribution programme. At its peak, around ten lakh—a million—people were being fed in over 1000 centres. I had been critical then of subjecting people to the indignity of having to line up for hours every day for a ladle of food. But although the food distribution could have been organized with more compassion and respect, it was still a crucial lifeline for the crores of people who had suddenly been put at risk of starvation. Now, with this lifeline snapped, there was nothing, except for a few small private charities which could not cope with the sheer magnitude of food deprivation.

My comrades working with homeless people in other cities across the country all reported conditions more grim and heart-breaking. There are also communities in the countryside—in forests, deserts, hills, river islands and Dalit ghettos—who even in normal times survived at the edge of hunger. They subsisted, barely, on remittances from migrants related to them; now *they* had to somehow feed the returned migrants. Casual daily-wage workers, weavers, artisans, home-based workers, rickshaw-pullers and street vendors—who have always lived a precarious existence—had slipped much deeper into want and poverty. And there were millions of new entrants into their ranks, including laid-off employees of micro and small factories, restaurants and little eateries, saloons and parlours; domestic workers, maalis, sex workers, drivers, press-walas, embroiderers, informal private nurses, teachers in low-income private schools and many, many others.

Months after the lockdown was lifted, these tens of millions are trying to cope with chronic hunger in ways that may be new to them but are hardwired into the DNA of the historically dispossessed. The first is to eliminate nutritious but unaffordable items from their diet, including dal, milk, vegetables, fruit, eggs and meat. Many families report that they are eating just rice and roti with salt. The next step is to reduce food intake, cutting down on both the number of meals per day and the quantity eaten at each meal, teaching the body to endure with less and less. There are increasing numbers of nights when they have to sleep hungry. Many children who earlier could depend on the school or pre-school centre for at least one nutritious meal are now sent out to work, including scrabbling through waste for anything that can be eaten or sold.

A UN study[71] warns that across the world 400 million (40 crore) new people are slipping into extreme poverty, of less than $1.90 a day, because of the economic impact of the pandemic and resulting lockdowns, and that this poverty will be considerably more severe. Around half of these new poor are in South Asia, mainly India. The economic impact is aggravated by 'pre-existing conditions of fragmented or insufficient social protection systems'. The UN Special Rapporteur on Extreme Poverty, Philip Alston, estimates that 'more than 250 million people are at risk of acute hunger'. This impoverishment, he believes, 'will be long-lasting', and he is critical of governments which 'rather than acknowledging how badly the efforts to "end poverty" have been faring, and how relentlessly the pandemic has exposed that fact…are doubling down on existing approaches that are clearly failing'.[72]

His criticism that public policies have failed massively to deal with the scale of the humanitarian crisis is entirely justified. There is, for instance, little acknowledgment of the extent and depth of the crisis in senior levels of the Indian government. Its relief package—involving new fiscal transfers of less than 1% of GDP in the first tranche and less than 2% overall—was one of the smallest in the world. To revive the economy and, in particular, MSMEs—the sector employing the most people outside agriculture—India's finance minister has relied mostly on credit rather than on fiscal transfers, unaware of the obvious fact, or unconcerned, that when both demand and production have crashed, credit will have few takers and can accomplish little.

It is hard to see this only as lack of competence; it is lack of will. After all, throughout one of the worst ever crises that we have faced, India's political establishment has displayed extraordinary industriousness in other matters—the buying and bullying of legislators in order to topple state governments, as in Madhya Pradesh, Rajasthan and Maharashtra; the purchase and televised worship of military aircraft; fabricating cases against and jailing dissenters; and pursuing divisive agendas like the triumphalist initiation of the construction of a Ram temple at the site of a demolished medieval mosque.

Meanwhile, crores of people have continued to sink invisibly into chronic and intense poverty.

*

A recurring, indeed the central, thesis of this book is that it would be a mistake to assume that the acute humanitarian crisis that is upon us was created by the deadly virus. It was the direct result of policy choices made by the central government to deal with the pandemic, mainly its decision to impose a nationwide lockdown, the largest and harshest on earth, but with one of the world's smallest relief packages. However, it is important to stress that this food, livelihood and public health catastrophe is not the consequence only of policies made *after* the pandemic hit us; it is also the cumulative consequence of profound public policy failures of the past several decades.

I can talk of many such failures, built on historically embedded oppressions of caste, tribe, gender and religious identity, and aggravated by India's political economy of neo-liberalism and elite capture. However, a triad of these policies have proved particularly disastrous for the working poor during and after the pandemic-induced lockdown. The first of these we will return to later in the book, namely the promotion of for-profit healthcare at the expense of public-health systems. The second is the near absence of food security for a significant proportion of the population. And the third is the state's failure to extend any substantive protection of labour rights and social security to nine out of ten workers in the country. I will examine the latter two in this chapter.

Food Security

The grossly under-reported and officially unacknowledged epidemic of food insecurity and hunger within just days of the lockdown resulted from India's chronically broken food security nets. Despite progressive Supreme Court rulings recognising the fundamental human right to food, the National Food Security Act of 2013, and a vibrant food rights people's campaign, India has not succeeded in the elementary duty of securing adequate, or even very basic, nutrition to all its people. Over a third of India's children are stunted and a fifth suffer from wasting.[73]

This widely known fact did not give the government pause when it decided to extinguish, for the majority of Indians, all possibilities of earning even the bare minimum needed for two decent meals a day. A report released by the Stranded Workers Action Network (SWAN)—as we have noted earlier—found that 50% of the 11,000 workers whom their volunteers contacted just three days after the lockdown had rations left for less than a day. Almost 96% had not received the promised government rations or any cooked food. And to compound their problems, 89% had not been paid by their employers who were, unsurprisingly, left entirely unmoved by the gentle, fleeting urgings of an otherwise firm and decisive prime minister. Of the workers surveyed across India by SWAN, 70% said they had less than 200 rupees left to survive the rest of the lockdown.[74]

When some state governments belatedly began to distribute cooked food and rations, large numbers of the

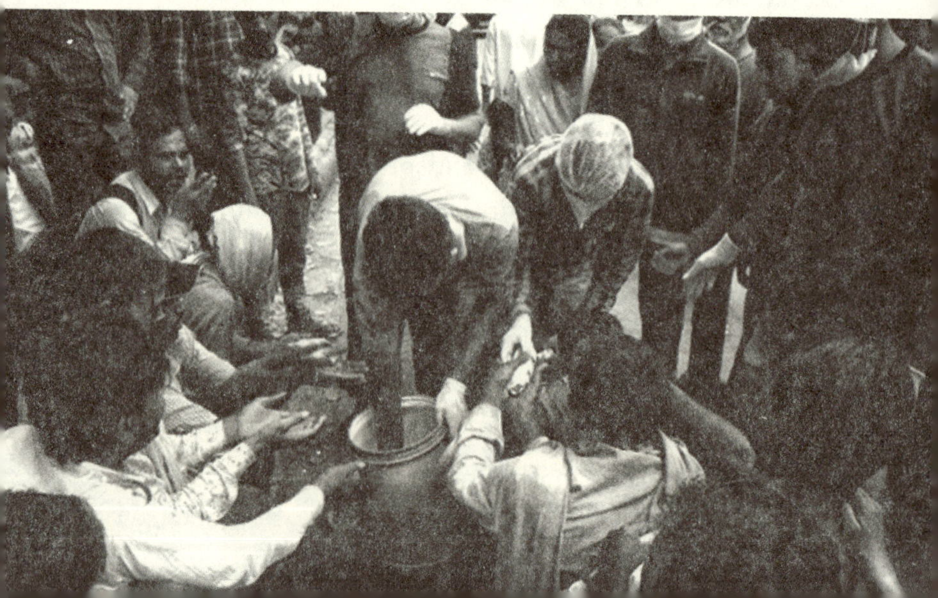

hungry slipped through the massive cracks which already riddled India's rudimentary food and social security protections. Food rights activists had for long pressed for a national network of community kitchens serving affordable and nutritious meals to informal workers, on the model of the Amma Canteens in Chennai. Had these been in place, they could have been pressed into service to feed the out-of-work labourers and their families, rather than making them stand in long lines on the road for cold food with little nutritional value and portions insufficient even for a young child.

Belatedly again, some state governments began distributing rations relying on the Public Distribution System (PDS). But circular seasonal migrants could not access the PDS because ration cards are not portable. Over the last 60 years one cornerstone of India's food security measures has been the distribution of subsidized cereals through the PDS. The National Food Security Act 2013 had made this a legal guarantee, ensuring that nearly 80 crore people would get at least half their calorie requirements almost for free. But economists Meghana Mungikar, Jean Drèze and Reetika Khera have estimated that 108.4 million people—almost 11 crore people—in India are excluded from the PDS.[75] Prabhat Patnaik underlines other gaps: 'First, not all essential commodities are distributed under the Public Distribution System; and second, not all the working people are covered by [it].'[76] Food rights activists have also long demanded a universal PDS, because any system of selection by the state of those who are most needy would always exclude those who are actually most food-vulnerable, because of their social and political powerlessness and invisibility. Particularly vulnerable to exclusion are migrant workers, who have no food rights outside their home states. Even when governments like those in Delhi introduced e-coupons for those who did not have ration cards, this still excluded those who didn't have access to smartphones through which to apply, and those without documents to prove that they were residents of Delhi—people who would also, naturally, be among the poorest, the most food-deprived. Again, had India established a universal PDS, it would have been the most effective vehicle to ward off mass hunger during the pandemic.

Labour Rights

Another of the many ironies of the development trajectory of the Indian republic is that informalisation of labour has grown in the periods of high economic growth over recent decades, especially after the economic liberalisation of 1991. Informal workers are those denied job security, statutory wages, safe and healthy working conditions and social security. Comprising 80 to 90 per cent of the Indian workforce, they engine the country's economy, contributing about half the GDP. They span most segments of the economy—agriculture, non-farm rural employment, construction, services and manufacturing, particularly in micro, small and medium units. But their work lives remain uncertain and extremely insecure. The 2007 report of the National Commission for Enterprises in the Unorganised Sector (NCEUS) highlighted that there is a strong overlap between India's historically marginalised groups—that are also trapped in the poorest economic quintiles of the country—and the phenomenon of informal work and seasonal and circular migration. The report notes: 'Scheduled Tribes, Scheduled Castes and religious minorities are trapped in low-wage livelihoods, with women and children within these social groups faring even worse.'[77]

Writing about the trials of the working poor when India was put under lockdown, economist and professor of development studies Barbara Harris-White marks out three broad segments of informal workers. She regards the lockdown as a 'declaration of war' by the Indian state on all three segments through its 'policy inaction'. The first segment she identifies are the migrant labourers, 'estimated as at least 20 million in urban areas alone', who were 'left to walk to their places of origin deprived of work, lodging and shelter, food, water and transport' or 'imprisoned in factory compounds and quarters, unpaid, poorly fed and prevented from returning home'.[78]

The second category Harris-White discusses is a much

larger segment of India's workforce hit by the lockdown, comprising the 'non-migrant self-employed, small family businesses and casual labour—perhaps as many as 350 million throughout the country'. Many among them are bypassed by the PDS, because state governments often are unwilling to accept them as permanent residents, while 'other government relief schemes, cash transfers and income support for vulnerable people are…inadequate and inaccessible…as though relief were deliberately intended to push households towards famine'.

And then Harris-White reminds us of 'India's vast unpaid workforce engaged in household production as well as domestic activity—perhaps in the region of 200 million—who are mostly women. The burden of maintaining the health of their households through this unprecedented income shock [of the lockdown]—redolent of triggers to famine processes—falls mostly on their backs.'

In two newspaper articles I wrote with economists Prabhat Patnaik and Jayati Ghosh on measures that we believed governments must take to mitigate the suffering created by the decimation of all livelihoods of workers, we advocated cash transfers of 7000 rupees a month to every household for at least three months, and universal access to PDS.[79] But while trying to spell out the details of how this could be actually operationalized, we encountered formidable problems for urban informal workers. Rural workers presented less of an operational challenge, thanks to the Mahatma Gandhi National Rural Employment Guarantee Programme, which ensures that all workers seeking wage employment in villages are registered with job cards and have bank accounts into which their wages are paid. But we realized that there is absolutely no reliable or even part-complete listing of informal workers in urban areas in any official records. The state has no system to ensure even the registration of migrant workers, meaning that they are invisible to the state. This is not a chance failure: it signifies that for decades the state has done nothing at all to secure the protection of the rights of urban informal workers or their social security, nor does it intend to do this. The only practical way we could find to emerge from this conundrum was to suggest—as conceived by Prabhat Patnaik—that any adult who presented herself or himself in designated offices in the city for the Rs 7000 cash transfer we were recommending, should be given the cash and a mark made with indelible ink (of the kind used during elections) on fingers assigned for each tranche of transfer. This crude and desperate stratagem underlined for us the enormity of the state's wilful abdication of its fundamental constitutional responsibilities to protect the rights of its vulnerable citizens.

It is not as though laws don't exist mandating the state to register migrant workers. The stated objective of the Interstate Migrant Workmen Act of 1979 is to regulate and lay down the conditions of service of circular migrant workers. It mandates registration of contractors who employ migrant workers and also requires all employers to maintain a record of their workers. However, by design itself, this excludes a vast majority of self-employed wage labourers and intra-state agrarian and other migrants in the informal economy. The 2011-12 report[80] of the Standing Committee on Labour records that 11 states do not have a single employer or contractor registered under this Act. The highest number of registered contractors and principal employers under the Act was in Bihar, but the figure were as absurdly low as 20 and 56 respectively. If reviewed and implemented in letter and spirit, this law would have made it much easier for the government to assist migrant workers during the lockdown. Unfortunately, that was not the case.

Similarly, the Building and Other Construction Workers (Regulation of Employment and Conditions of Service) Act, 1996, or BOCW, acknowledges the seasonality and precarious nature of employment of construction workers and defines anyone who has worked in construction for at least 90 days in the past year as a construction worker. This law makes registered establishments responsible for providing housing and child care facilities to such workers and obliges state construction boards to register workers as beneficiaries of several welfare measures. However, each worker needs the employer or a trade union to certify her or him to be a construction worker in order to avail these benefits. The lived reality of a large section of informal workers is that they are deliberately overlooked by this legislation. They keep migrating from place to place and are largely non-unionised and undocumented. A recent study conducted by Jan Sahas found that more than 90% of the construction workers they interviewed were outside the ambit of this act since they did not have BOCW cards. And only 29% of the small number of 20.37 lakh labourers registered under the BOCW Board in Uttar Pradesh had access to a bank account.[81]

Both BOCWA and the Inter-State Migrant Act require the following: Workers should be registered at source, employers should maintain registers of workers at construction sites, and there should be a record of the workers in the state labour department. However, there is nothing in the law, or in practice, to hold the state and industry accountable in this regard. Labour departments are chronically understaffed and notoriously corrupt. The 2018 annual report of the Department of Labour in Karnataka, for instance, reveals that it had only 23 sanctioned staff (of which nine posts lay vacant), and was responsible for implementing BOCWA, in addition to other labour laws across all 30 districts in the state.[82]

Aaditeshwar Seth, co-founder of Gram Vaani, a Delhi-based social enterprise, explained to *India Spend*: 'Although the enforcement of labour laws even for documented workers has been weak, a significant reason why worker rights are often violated is a heavily undocumented workforce.' He said that on the one hand, complex self-registration processes deter workers from registering. These include elaborate documentation, filling of detailed forms, proof of employment, registration with the state worker welfare boards, all of which powerless, impoverished and often poorly lettered workers find very difficult. He also explained why employers are motivated to under-report the number of workers they employ—it allows them to save on mandatory costs for social-security payments per employee and costs for employee benefits (such as transportation and living expenses). At the same time, it helps them to avail of benefits for units with less workers than the thresholds set under various laws pertaining to factories, industry, unionisation and so on. 'This means that they [workers] are invisible—the government does not know who they are and they are unable to claim any insurance benefits, maternity benefits, housing, and other provisions allowed under such schemes.' Rajiv Khandelwal, executive director of Aajeevika Bureau, an agency working for communities dependent on migration and labour, added, 'The result of this invisibility is not restricted to just cash transfers. It also makes it easier for employers to forego their obligations.'[83]

To this decades-long history of unconscionable neglect of the labour rights of India's informal workers, various states added a shocking new dimension. Many state governments tried to use the pandemic to further weaken even the feeble protections that the law currently provides, including an (ultimately unsuccessful) bid to extend the work-day to 12 hours, and to control the movement of workers across state borders.

The governments of Gujarat, Madhya Pradesh and Himachal Pradesh cited the public emergency (of the pandemic) to extend maximum hours of work to 12 hours a day and 72 hours a week, followed by the governments of Odisha, Maharashtra and Goa.[84] Uttar Pradesh went further, proposing an ordinance to suspend almost all labour laws for factories and manufacturing establishments in the state for three years.[85] Gujarat signalled its resolve to follow the example of Uttar Pradesh. Madhya Pradesh diluted provisions of the Factories Act[86], which enjoins employers to ensure health, safety, fair remuneration and welfare of the workers, and Karnataka freed many establishments from the application of various labour laws.[87]

The Madhya Pradesh government also gave the go ahead to changes in the Contract Labour (Regulation and Abolition) Act 1970 and the Industrial Disputes Act 1947, which actually were already in the pipeline. For instance, the move to allow government approved Third Party Inspectors, as opposed to Government Inspectors, to provide certification to non-hazardous units employing up to 50 persons, was part of the Business Reform Action Plan of 2016 charted out by the Union Ministry of Commerce and Industries. So were the changes in the Contract Labour (Regulation and Abolition) Act. The more significant changes introduced by the MP government pertain to relations between labour and management and dispute resolution.[88] In one stroke the mechanisms which sought to protect labour from exploitative employers have been all but dismantled. For instance, the comprehensive infrastructure provided by the Industrial Disputes Act 1947—with labour courts and tribunals to sort out disputes pertaining to retrenchment, strikes and unfair labour practices—has been made ineffective through the provision that all industries to be set up within 1000 days of the notification will be exempted from adhering to this law.[89] Similarly, the decision[90] of the MP government to exempt key labour intensive industries from the purview of the Madhya Pradesh Industrial Relations Act 1960 (MPIRA) undermines the mechanisms of ensuring accountability of the employers.[91] The MPIRA recognizes, among other rights, the right of labourers to represent themselves through unions. The suspension of this Act with regards to industries like textiles, iron and steel, sugar, cement, electrical goods, transport etc, will have drastic implications for trade unions and labour rights.

While the MP government at least made a pretence of retaining some minimum safeguards pertaining to workers' safety, retrenchment and payment for overtime, the government of Uttar Pradesh did not bother itself with even such cosmetic concerns. In its Uttar Pradesh Temporary Exemption from Certain Labour Laws Ordinance 2020, it did away with almost all labour laws in their entirety.[92]

The stated reason for this sweeping move was that industry needed a push and investment had to be brought in to revive the economic health of the state and generate employment after the lockdown. The only exceptions to the almost total suspension of labour laws in the state were the Building and Other Construction Workers Act, 1996, Workmen Compensation Act, 1923, the Bonded Labour Act, 1976 and portions of the Payment of Wages Act, 1936. The UP government also extended working hours to 12 per day, but the payment for overtime was kept at the same rate as the usual working hours, in contrast to the double rate prescribed in the Factories Act, 1948. In effect, the labouring population in UP is now bereft of all provisions that had previously, at least on paper, ensured their safety, health, welfare benefits like resting places and washrooms, job security, and the right to unionize.

In the same vein, the government of Gujarat announced 'exemption for new industrial projects from Labour Laws except provisions for minimum wages, safety and compensation in case of accidents.'[93] In April itself, the Gujarat government had announced that working hours could be extended to 12 per day without the payment of overtime double rate of wages for the next three months.[94]

The withdrawal of labour law protections is not limited to BJP-ruled states. Congress-ruled states like Rajasthan also increased the number of working hours to 12 per day.[95] Punjab too, in an order dated 20 April,[96] increased the daily working hours to 12, albeit with double the rate of usual wages for overtime. And there are reports, at the time of writing, that Punjab is mulling a loosening of its labour regime along the lines of what has been done in UP, Gujarat and MP.[97]

Some of these changes, particularly the extension of the workday to 12 hours, have been blocked by legal challenges. The central government, tellingly, made no intervention.

Just as the Indian state excluded the labouring poor from its public health strategy during the pandemic by imposing a lockdown to ensure 'social distancing' which protected only the middle classes, it now seeks to revive the broken economy by excluding desperate, vulnerable workers from labour rights protections, thus further legitimising what Alpa Shah and Jens Lerche describe as their super-exploitation'[98].

7

Lockdown, Government 'Packages' and the Supreme Court

A week into the lockdown, lawyers Prashant Bhushan and Cheryl D'Souza filed a public interest petition in the Supreme Court, seeking the upholding of the right to life with dignity under Article 21 of the Constitution for the migrants who were badly hit by the lockdown. The petitioners were Anjali Bhardwaj and this writer.

In the course of one of the hearings on the 7th of April 2020, the Chief Justice of India observed that since the workers were being provided meals by the government, why would they need money!

Our petition had pointed to the intense humanitarian crisis created by the lockdown, and its central demand was that the central and state governments must 'jointly and severally' ensure payment of minimum wages to all migrant workers within a week for the entire period of the lockdown. This, the petition said, should be irrespective of whether they were employed in an establishment, engaged by contractors, or self-employed. Our petition also demanded that this must be done by self-attestation and self-identification, because the state has no comprehensive record of employed workers, let alone casual and self-employed workers. Our application to the court detailed what we saw as serious flaws and inadequacies in the union government's response to the devastating impact of its lockdown strategy on the livelihoods and food security of the working poor.

Prime Minister Narendra Modi had only tersely mentioned the poor in his first address to the country announcing the lockdown. He had said, 'This crisis has certainly brought on a very difficult time for the poor. Along with the central and state governments, individuals from civil societies and institutions are constantly striving to reduce the problems of the poor. Several people are collaborating their efforts to help the poor.'[99] No specific measures did he spell out for people who were about to be hit by a tsunami of dispossession and suffering created by the hand of the state. It seemed that for the prime minister it was mainly the duty of civil society to mitigate the workers' distress, as though their survival in a catastrophe entirely not of their making was a matter to be mitigated by private charity; the state had no responsibility towards them. In his later address signalling the extension of the lockdown, Modi appealed to employers to pay their workers and to landlords to not demand rent payments,[100] again signalling that workers should depend on charity and benevolence, this time of their employers and landlords, rather than their rights as equal citizens of the republic.

A few days after the lockdown, Finance Minister Nirmala Sitharaman announced a relief package.[101] Her objective, she declared, was to shield the poor from the economic impact of the Coronavirus shutdown. 'No one will go hungry,' she promised. Did she really believe that five extra kilos of wheat or rice and one kilo of pulses for families with ration cards, Rs 1,000 for the aged, disabled and widows, Rs 1,500 over three months for women with Jan Dhan (or no-frills) bank accounts, free gas cylinders for three months and a Rs 2,000 cash transfer to farmers under an already on-going scheme, would ensure this? 'People also need cash,' Sitharaman had said gravely, magnanimously, explaining why the government was making cash transfers of 500 rupees a month, for three months, for women. Had someone done the math for her? Rs 500 amounts to less than one and a half days' minimum wages. And this too was being given only to those with active and operational Jan Dhan bank accounts. Think if you and I were told that we have to survive on less than two-days' salary and six kilos of grain a month, and with no health insurance. What would the repeatedly-extending lockdown look like to us in such a case?

Only once in his successive addresses to the nation on measures to fight the spread of COVID-19, after tens of thousands of migrant workers had trudged hundreds of kilometres, many losing their lives along the way, did the prime minister in passing express regret. In a *Mann ki baat* broadcast a week into the lockdown, the PM sought forgiveness from the poor people: 'I specially ask for their forgiveness…I understand your troubles. But there was no other way to protect a country of 1.3 billion such as India from the dangerous effects of Coronavirus. The fight against Corona is one between life and death and we have to win it.'[102] He sought their forgiveness, but did not offer them redressal or redemption from state-induced suffering. It was still early in the lockdown and relief measures at that time could have prevented to an extent the vast human crisis that was to unfold. In an open letter to Indians on the anniversary of his second term as PM, he said, 'Our labourers, migrant workers, artisans and craftsmen in small scale industries, hawkers and such fellow countrymen have undergone tremendous suffering. We are working in a united and determined way to alleviate their troubles.'[103] And yet the letter preoccupied itself mainly with the resolve to make India self-reliant (*atmanirbhar*) and spoke of the glorious future that awaited her, rather than outlining concrete ways to lift the labouring poor from the unprecedented health and humanitarian crisis into which they had been thrust.

In July the PM announced that the free rations promised by his finance minister in late March would now be available to ration card holders until November. He rhetorically declared, 'Let there not be a single home in which the hearth is not burning.'[104] This was welcome, but too little for the levels of food and work distress that had been unleashed. We have already noted that many of the most vulnerable households don't have ration cards. Also, this measure did not benefit migrants who faced the severest disruptions after the lockdown. The finance minister belatedly, on May 14, announced five kilos of free grains for migrants as well, for two months. But the government's own data showed that by 30 June, only 13% of this grain had been distributed to the migrants by the states.[105] The disinterest of the states was perhaps because the migrants are not voters in their destination states. (This strengthens the case both for a universal PDS, and for national portability of voting rights. If migrants were allowed to vote wherever they were on voting day, state governments would not be so indifferent to their suffering.)

The overall tight-fistedness of the union government in distributing food grain far more expansively—in order to provide meaningful relief, and not as insulting tokenism—is even more culpable when we consider that as of March 2020, the Food Corporation of India held 77 million (7.7 crore) tonnes of rice and wheat stocks, which is more than *three times* the required buffer stock. By late June, after the rabi harvest for the year, the stocks had grown to 100 million tonnes, four times the required buffer stock. The average of the three years immediately preceding 2020 shows that the PDS needs about 54 million tonnes of food grain to ensure provisions to all ration-card holders in the country for one full year. Development economist Jean Dreze estimates that only an additional 20 million tonnes would be needed to universalise the system for one year.[106] It is criminal that the government will not distribute grains to the public when much grain is being wasted in storage, and costs of storage are higher than the costs of distributing the grain.

In response to our petition to the Supreme Court, the union government reported to the Court that it had announced a financial package of Rs. 1.70 lakh crores. We replied that the package, just around 1% of GDP, was entirely inadequate to deal with the crisis. Further, many elements of the scheme were merely front-loading instalments of existing schemes, such as a daily wage increase under MGNREGA, or emergency support through the Building and Other Construction Workers' (BOCW) Cess funds. The five kilos of grains and one kilo of pulses would not reach a large section of migrant workers, as PDS is a domicile-based entitlement which requires proof of permanent address. The ex-gratia of Rs 500 each to 20.4 crore women with Jan Dhan accounts was also extremely inadequate—in fact, a travesty of assistance—both in terms of quantum and the inclusion only of those women with functional bank accounts.[107]

The union government claimed in its reply that its financial package took care of the daily needs of every poor person, including migrant workers and their families, and that there was no imperative for migrant workers to rush to their villages.[108] Their daily needs were being taken care of wherever they were working, and the needs of their families were being assured in the villages. It added that the central government had directed states to provide food, shelter and medical facilities to migrant workers who had been quarantined en route to their places of origin.[109]

We contested all of this as well. Even the figures of the number of active relief camps and shelters for migrant workers released by the government laid bare the complete inadequacy of the official provisions made for migrants. In a release issued by the government's Press Information Bureau (PIB) a week after the lockdown began, the union home ministry claimed that '21,486 relief camps have been set up, in which 6,75,133 persons are being provided shelter, and around 25 lakhs are being provided meals.'[110] Estimates on the number of migrant workers across India range from 4 crores to 15 crores—40 to 150 million. Even if the lower end of the estimate is used, i.e., 4 crores, 25 lakh workers would account for just 6% of the migrant labour force—when the lockdown had put *all* of them out of work and all of them were in need of food support.

In the Supreme Court, the government submitted that there were 26,476 active relief camps and shelters in which 10,37,027 persons were housed. But it did not reveal that

Kerala alone accounted for 59% of these camps and shelters. And just two states, Haryana and Delhi, accounted for 51% of the 15 lakh people who the union government said were being given cooked food.[111]

Our petition also spoke of problems with the order of 29 March of the union government, under the Disaster Management Act 2005, which directed all public and private employers to continue paying workers their wages through the period of the lockdown. This order also prescribed that landlords should not seek rent from workers during the period. We argued first that this in effect shifted the entire burden of protecting the migrant workers' earnings and preventing their eviction from rented homes away from the state and on to the shoulders of employers and landlords. Many of them were themselves very small entrepreneurs and property-owners and did not have the capacity (nor the moral responsibility) to bear these costs of a lockdown imposed by the state. Besides, the order instituted no mechanism to secure its implementation, nor for redress when it was flouted.

Further, this order made no provision for the financial security of the large proportion of migrant workers who are self-employed and are therefore not paid any salaries, such as street vendors, rickshaw-pullers, dhobis, petty service providers, rag-pickers and sex workers. It also ignored completely one of the most vulnerable segments of the labour market, namely casual daily-wage workers. Studies show that only 17% of workers in the informal sector have identifiable employers.[112] The earnings of the remaining 83% would not be protected even if every employer obeyed the 29 March order. And all surveys of migrant workers establish that very few heeded the sermon of the Prime Minister to pay wages during the lockdown.[113]

The Supreme Court bench stated that in times of such crisis it did not want to interfere with government decisions—which begs the question: when exactly is the intervention of the country's highest institution for justice most necessary, if not in times of crisis? On complaints raised by our lawyer Prashant Bhushan about inedible food in crowded shelters or the lack of access to food at the feeding centres opened by the government, the Court merely asked the government to put in place a helpline for complaints.[114]

Into the third phase of the lockdown, the prime minister announced a grand relief package of 20 lakh crore rupees, calling it 'Atmanirbhar Bharat Abhiyan' (Self-reliant India Mission) and claiming that it amounted to 10% of the GDP. This kindled brief hopes of belated succour for the labouring poor. But it turned out to be one more of the conjuring tricks that the Indian people have come to associate with Prime Minister Modi, because it was revealed that there was only around 1% of the GDP of *new public spending* in this package, and there was even less than this for the poor. About 99% of what was being described as a grand package was what had already been announced, plus the measures that the Reserve Bank of India had taken to infuse liquidity into the banking system. Analysts found that the largest part of the package was credit-focussed, aimed at easing liquidity problems of various enterprises, and would be paid out by banks. *The Wire* examined estimates by a number of economists and market experts of the fiscal impact of the package and found that in real terms the additional and direct fiscal spending would be less than Rs 2.5 lakh crore—a little over 1% of GDP—even by the most optimistic calculations. Conservative, and perhaps more realistic, calculations put it at 1.5 lakh crore—0.7% of GDP.[115] Most countries have committed much larger shares of their GDP to relief for people stricken by the pandemic and consequent lockdowns. For instance, among countries with comparable infection case-loads or economies, Brazil contributed 11.8%, China 7%, United States 13.2%, Turkey 10.8% and Japan 21.1% of their GDPs.

In addition to spending, the quality of leadership seems to have had an effect on the containment strategies. India's official communication was stymied first because Prime Minister Modi believes only in one-way communication, never fielding questions in an open press-conference. He will probably hold the record of the only head of state in the world who did not address a single press conference during the COVID-19 pandemic.[116] This contrasts with heads of governments in countries which best handled the pandemic. It is interesting that most of these countries are led by women, whether Germany, New Zealand, Denmark, Finland or Taiwan. They continuously conversed with their people, explaining every decision; an example also followed by the chief minister and health minister of Kerala. They went out of the way to explain the rationale of every restriction, did not hide the dangers but explained what steps they were taking and communicated empathy for the difficulties these were causing. They answered questions and doubts patiently. Not surprisingly, New Zealand had extraordinary success in containing the spread of the virus, at a time when infections were mounting dangerously every day in countries led by 'strongmen'—the United States, India, Brazil, Russia and the United Kingdom.

The contrast between New Zealand and India is very instructive. The New Zealand prime minister held daily briefings, and rather than spur fear or stigmatize communities, as was done in India, she advocated (and practiced) a 'kindness-first' approach. Both countries imposed their lockdowns at around the same time. But by early May, New Zealand was able to announce no new cases of COVID-19 for 100 days, whereas India at the same time had infection rates soaring dizzyingly.[117] *Lancet* identified two reasons for New Zealand's remarkable success. One was its very high levels of testing, with more than 150,000 people tested in a country of just 5 million (50 lakh). Testing focused on symptomatic persons, and both close contacts and casual contacts; followed by more widespread testing. The second reason was the response which 'placed science, leadership and careful language at the forefront'. Siouxsie Wiles, a microbiologist and science communicator, underlined the way in which COVID-19 was framed to the general population in New Zealand. 'In other countries, people have been talking about war and battle, which puts people in a negative and fearful frame of mind,' she said. 'The official response here has been guided by the principle that you do not stigmatise and that we unite against COVID-19. [Prime Minister] Ardern has regularly appeared on social media, smiling and sharing parts of her personal life under lockdown but without underplaying the seriousness of the situation, which has helped to build public trust.'[118]

Almost everything the Indian government said and did, however, achieved exactly the opposite of building trust and encouraging public empathy and solidarity by example. In late March, the Solicitor General of India said in the Supreme Court that the massive exodus of migrant workers was merely the result of rumours and 'fake news'—thus not only refusing to acknowledge the suffering of the workers but, in effect, calling it a lie. Although he did not offer any evidence to support his outrageous statement, it was accepted by the Chief Justice, who said that 'it is not possible for us to ignore this menace of fake news either by electronic, print or social media'.

Six months later, when asked for reasons for the migrant crisis in the first session of Parliament convened after the lockdown, the union minister of state for home fell back on this same alibi of 'fake news'. He replied that the lockdown was imposed to 'stop the untraceable movement of people from one place to another within the country'! He claimed that the government had made adequate arrangements to ensure all basic amenities—food, water, medical care—to all people, but misinformation was spread that these amenities would run out. The mass migration, he said, was 'triggered by panic created by fake news' about the duration of the lockdown and that essential supplies to migrant workers may run short. The minister would not admit that the fear and panic about how long the lockdown would last were caused by the repeated extensions by the government, without any advance warning or explanation, and theatrically announced by a leader who had infantilised the entire country, positioning himself as the supreme patriarch who always knew best, who could not be questioned, advised or guided. The minister would not admit that beyond the fortified bungalows and hushed lawns that people like him inhabited, many millions were at the mercy of charities for a little food and water; millions were making terrible journeys on foot to the tenuous security of their impoverished village homes, and many of them were dying in the process. The minister denied all of this, even though he admitted he had no data about the numbers of non-COVID deaths among migrants, the compensation promised for the families of lockdown victims, or jobs lost during the lockdown.[119]

In the final hearing of our petition in the Supreme Court, a newly constituted bench of the Court heard the case very briefly. In this hearing, the petitioners additionally placed on record the study by the Stranded Workers Action Network—SWAN—(referred to earlier in the book) which had found alarming conditions of hunger among migrant workers just days after the lockdown was announced.[120] But the Court was still not persuaded by the huge and credible evidence of destitution and hunger which, our lawyers informed them, was mounting dangerously with every day of the court hearings. The bench said it could not rely on studies by private bodies when the government portrayed a completely different picture. The government painted this 'different picture' with no evidence at all, but this did not seem to matter.

And so the Supreme Court of India chose to finally close the case, without giving any relief to the migrants during the lockdown. The final order blandly read: 'We call upon the respondent, Union of India, to look into such material and take such steps as it finds fit to resolve the issues raised in the petition.'[121]

For the crores of migrant workers stranded in cities without work and food, or confined to overcrowded and underserved shelters, or walking endlessly on burning highways across the country, or despairing in their villages in conditions of enormous economic distress, the prospect of a life of basic security and dignity became even more remote.

8

Costs of the Lockdown

On 15 October 2020, a 16-year-old boy hanged himself from the roof of his small home in a village called Pal in Goa. The smartphone that he and his brother used to attend online classes—since schools were still shut—had broken and needed to be repaired. It was the only smartphone the family owned, and repairing it would cost 2000 rupees.

The boy's father drove a private bus, and used to earn 700 rupees a day. After the lockdown, there was no income for four months. Since July he had been able to work, but earned about 500 rupees, and even that on good days. His wife was a beneficiary of Goa's Griha Aadhar Scheme but had received just one payment of Rs 1,500 in the seven months since the lockdown because the state said it had little money left. When the young boy asked his father for the money to repair the phone, something broke in the older man. 'We had been struggling for months so everyone was in a bad mood,' the father told Smita Nair of *The Indian Express*. 'He got into an argument with me and I held him by the collar. He stopped me saying, "I have only one nice shirt." He removed his shirt, put it on a hanger and told me I could beat him. By then I just couldn't…I then told him I only had 500 rupees with me and needed it to buy rice. I asked him to wait for four days for me to arrange the Rs 2,000.' When the boy hanged himself, his parents were broken. They had never cut corners for their children's education, but what could they do when they earned barely enough now to feed the family? Their boy was a diligent student, he used to say he would become a big man one day and help them. 'The government says study online, but can poor people afford these phones? The government should pause schooling for a year if they cannot help the poor,' the father said to Nair. 'Please mention the plight of us poor people…When [we are] in need, there is no help.'[122]

One of India's most thoughtful legal philosophers, Upendra Baxi, observes that the tacit assumption behind many of the harsh official anti-COVID-19 strategies has been that some imposed suffering is a necessary evil and 'bearing it gracefully (is) considered as a badge of national unity and patriotism'. But he insists that some suffering must be classified as 'surplus' or unnecessary suffering. This unnecessary suffering occurs 'when every individual person is regarded as a potential carrier of disease and exposed to state and social control and management.' Is sheer survival to be considered paramount in the management of a global pandemic, with all constitutional values deemed secondary in the process? 'Or, should it also be the case,' he asks, 'that anti-COVID-19 performances must not violate basic human rights? For example, the human right to health may not be held incompatible with the human right to live with dignity[.]'[123]

Since the lockdown was justified by its supporters

primarily as the surest recourse to save human lives, to evaluate the success of deploying this ultimate 'weapon' in the public health arsenal we need a careful evaluation of its accomplishments weighed against its costs. In the most elementary terms, how many lives did the lockdown save, and how many lives has it taken away or destroyed—and will continue to destroy? It is too early to do a full assessment of the cost of the lockdown in terms of the loss of human lives, because there is still little data transparency and hardly any detailed studies available, but what we already know is devastating.

But first, what has the lockdown done to the economy?

Economic Costs of the Lockdown

India was already struggling with a serious economic downturn when the shutting down of both demand and supply across the country overnight led to a calamitous shrinkage of the economy. Surajit Das, an economist from JNU, calculated that even assuming government consumption remained unaffected and private consumption expenditure was one third of normal during the lockdown period, in 40 days of lockdown, private consumption would have fallen by 9 lakh crore rupees. Since capital or investment is unlikely during a lockdown, investment demand would have fallen by at least 6.75 lakh crore rupees. Adding the trade deficit, the net loss in GDP due to lockdown would have been to the tune of 16 lakh crore rupees. This is equivalent to 8% of the current GDP of India.[124] The estimates of Tejal Kaniktar, Associate Professor at the National Institute of Advanced Studies, are even more dire. He expects that the total loss of output would to be between 40 and 66 lakh crore rupees, or about 20 to 32% of the GDP.[125]

Veteran journalist and economist Prem Shankar Jha points out that India's five crore (50 million) micro, small and medium enterprises—which form the bulwark of the entire economy, contributing, by official estimates, over one-third of exports and around half the national income—have been hit hardest by the lockdown. These units employ over 11 crore (110 million) workers; outside agriculture, the largest number of Indians are sustained by this sector. When all activity stopped due to the complete and drastic countrywide lockdown, these enterprises came to a standstill. Quoting from the weekly survey of employment of the Centre for Monitoring Indian Economy (CMIE), Jha writes, '114 million workers, almost half of the non-agricultural workforce, were out of work in April, of whom 91 million are daily wage earners and 17 million are salary earners. At a conservative estimate, their lost income amounts to Rs 90,000 crore a month. That is the extent of the decline in demand from this sector alone.'[126] Spread across the country, down to tehsils and villages, small enterprises survive on modest to tiny turnovers. It is estimated that 98.6% of the five crore MSMEs employ less than 10 workers, of which 95% employ less than five workers. They are critical for the survival of the vast majority of the working poor outside agriculture and construction.

A June report of the Global Alliance for Mass Entrepreneurship pointed out that even in normal times many MSMEs were 'perennially stuck in a vicious cycle of informality, low productivity' and 'remain stunted'. The government's main support to MSMEs after the unimaginable destruction of the lockdown was to create a special credit line for them. But more credit to MSMEs is hardly helpful when there are massive and severe constraints on both demand and supply. The GAME Report makes a grim forecast, that 'COVID-19 could become a mass-extinction event for smaller, informal firms', and that 30% to 40% of MSMEs in India may be extinguished during the pandemic.[127]

The impact on women migrants is even more damaging and more invisible. Aajeevika Bureau found that in Ahmedabad, a textiles centre, women are employed as home-based workers by domestic and global businesses. Even before the pandemic, the women were earning an average daily wage of as little as Rs 40 to Rs 50, without any basic labour rights, including food, shelter, wage, health and employment security. After the lockdown, they are earning as little as Rs 10 to Rs 15. One reason they continue to work even for this pittance is to escape the violence of their husbands if they are unable to bring any food to the table. Moreover, they cannot afford to lose their links with the contractors who bring them this work.[128] Feminist economist Ashwini Deshpande found a highly unequal impact of job losses due to the lockdown on women's employment. The Indian economy has been seeing the decline of women's employment for many years. But even starting from this low base, Deshpande estimates that four out of ten women who were in paid jobs last year have lost their work during the lockdown.

For Dalits, too, Deshpande estimates, job losses have been three times higher than for the general caste worker, because people of these advantaged castes tend to have higher access to education and therefor to relatively more secure jobs in the formal economy which has been less drastically hit. But she adds, 'While women and Dalits have suffered disproportionately more job losses, risky, hazardous and stigmatized jobs are exclusively their preserve. All frontline health workers are women; manual scavengers are exclusively Dalit. Thus, for several women and Dalits, the choice seems to be between unemployment and jobs that put them at risk of disease and infection and make them targets of vicious stigma.'[129]

The Centre for Monitoring Indian Economy (CMIE), an independent body, has compiled very worrying data indicating major job losses even for salaried workers in the formal sector of the economy during the COVID-19 lockdown. In April, the month immediately following the lockdown, 17.7 million (1.77 crore) salaried jobs were lost; 0.1 million jobs were lost in May; a recovery of 3.9 million jobs in June, and then again a loss of 5 million jobs in July—so a total net loss of 18.9 million jobs in four months. 'While salaried jobs are not lost easily, once lost they are also far more difficult to retrieve,' noted the report. 'Therefore, their ballooning numbers are a source of worry. Salaried jobs were nearly 19 million short of their average in 2019-20.'[130]

Economist Jayan Jose Thomas of IIT Delhi has calculated that income losses by vulnerable sections of India's workforce during the two months of the lockdown were as much as four lakh crore rupees. Jose identifies casual workers, the poorest 60% among the self-employed, and regular workers who do not receive social security benefits as the most vulnerable of India's workers. Azim Premji University's Centre for Sustainable Employment estimated that 80% of urban workers lost their jobs while farmers and self-employed workers suffered huge income falls. Other surveys showed that a substantial proportion of these workers did not even receive the salaries they had been due to receive for the month of March 2020.[131]

We must always bear in mind that the economic cost of a lockdown is much higher for the poor. Their numbers have risen hugely due to the lockdown, and will continue to swell. Definitions of poverty are controversial among economists and policy-makers, but few would deny that significant segments of the Indian population are poor or close to poverty, and in addition there are large numbers who are vulnerable to a fall into poverty in hard times. Ninety per cent of India's workers are informal, and at least 70% of them would be economically fragile, unable to bear the shocks of the lockdown and consequent loss of jobs. Development economist K.P. Kannan reminds us of the intense vulnerability of India's working poor. In 2018, 80% of the country's 461 million (46.1 crore) workers were employed in the informal sector, such as in agricultural work and in MSMEs. Almost 49 million of the remaining 92 million workers in the formal sector are employed as temporary, informal workers. About 52% of all workers—238 million—are self-employed; 24%, or 112 million, are casual labour. Kannan underlines that the majority of workers who contribute to the making of the national income belong to the category of the working poor, a staggering 369 million workers. He also points to an official 2019 report of the Ministry of Labour and Employment which estimated that nearly two out of three informal workers, totalling 278 million, do not even earn the Rs. 375 a day recommended by the government as the minimum wage necessary to meet the most basic household needs at 2017-18 prices.

Kannan stresses that even without the assault of the lockdown, most of these working poor 'negotiate their daily needs through uncertain livelihood opportunities that make them, in the words of humanist-sociologist Jan Breman… "wage hunters and gatherers" and "footloose labourers".' Who are these people, he asks? 'Think of the millions of agricultural labourers and poor peasants producing food grains and processed foods for those who have the money to buy them at will; hewers of wood and drawers of water; workers who load and unload goods at scattered points of trade and commerce across our vast nation; rickshaw pullers in towns and cities coming from distant villages; barbers and washer(wo)men, manual scavengers and garbage pickers, street vendors and domestic servants, auto rickshaw and taxi drivers, brick kiln workers and construction workers who migrate from villages to cities and towns in search of work, workers in repair shops and small workshops producing all kinds of cheap consumer articles and consumer durables that end up in corporate warehouses, roadside eatery workers and those in small hotels and restaurants, "security staff" who protect the middle class and the rich in their gated habitats, delivery workers who deliver food and e-commerce packages at the doorsteps of millions of homes and companies, and similar umpteen groups of workers bracketed under the informal sector status.'[132]

A survey by Gaon Connection and the Centre for Study of Developing Societies underlined enormous rural distress as well. About 35% families went without food the whole day either many times or sometimes, 38% skipped an entire meal in a day several times or sometimes, and 46% reduced a few items from their meal often or sometimes. It found that over 68% of rural Indians were in a monetary crisis while 78% found the work that gave them an income coming to a complete standstill; 23% of the respondents had to borrow money to manage their household, while 8% had to sell a valuable possession like a mobile phone or a watch. Close to a fourth of the migrant workers who had fled cities to escape job loss and the pandemic said they'd had to walk back home. Only a fifth of them had found work under the rural employment guarantee scheme.[133]

By the end of August, extremely grim data about the state of the economy came in from official sources. The Ministry of Statistics and Programme Implementation reported that India's GDP growth rate had contracted by 23.9% for the April to June quarter. Even this was likely to be a significant under-estimate, because the data excludes the condition of the informal sector, which was worst hit by the lockdown. This is the worst contraction in recorded history, and indeed the first time in four decades that India has experienced an economic contraction.[134] India's first Chief Statistician and leading economist Pronab Sen believes that if the informal sector is factored in, the contraction could be even higher, as much as 33%. He says the situation is grim and likely to get worse—his estimate is that India's GDP will likely shrink over 10% by March 2021.

Vivek Kaul, an economics and finance writer, said to *Scroll* that the situation in India 'is much worse than [in] every other large economy in the world'. The reason, he said, was that Prime Minister Narendra Modi imposed the lockdown 'very quickly, without thinking it through'. Other industrialized countries which resorted to a lockdown have also experienced contractions, but none as severe as in India. In the United States the contraction was 9.1%, in the United Kingdom 21.7%, in Japan 9.9% whereas China has actually shown a growth of 3.2%.[135]

The sectors which are worst hit are: construction (at 50.3%), manufacturing and trade (39.3%), and hotels and transport (47.0%).[136] This is particularly worrying, because outside agriculture these are the sectors which account for the highest employment of both formal and informal workers.

But the government remains in denial. Finance minister Nirmala Sitharaman calls the contraction 'an act of god'.

Economists with political beliefs across the spectrum from left to right—except those fiscal conservatives who seem to have the highest influence on the union government and believe that even in an unprecedented crisis of this magnitude, government must keep its fiscal deficit low—are convinced that the only hope for some revival of the economy even in the medium-run would require massive public spending, of the kind Keynesians recommended in the New Deal to overcome the Great Depression in America in the 1930s. If large universal cash transfers to every household and universal PDS had been deployed from the start of the lockdown, the human costs would have been reduced significantly and the prospects for economic recovery enhanced. But policy-makers in the PMO and South Block seem still in the throes of neo-liberal fiscal conservatism, which in times of a crisis of such depth is nothing short of suicidal.

Health and Human Costs of the Lockdown

Economist S.A. Aiyar makes important global comparisons of the health and human costs of lockdowns and concludes that across the world this drastic measure may be taking almost as many lives as COVID-19.[137] He quotes a comparison by the *Financial Times*, London of excess mortality in March and April—the excess of deaths over the average for five preceding years—for several countries. The paper found excess mortality as high as 49%. In Europe, it was highest in Belgium and the Netherlands, at 60% and 51% respectively. Sweden, on the other hand, the only European country which refused to lock down, had a figure of only 12%. Since the lockdown would have substantially reduced deaths from traffic and workplace accidents and homicides, mortality should in fact have come down, instead of this steep spike. So what explains the excess mortality? Clearly, the side effects of the lockdown.

Lockdown deaths could have been caused by the diversion of health-care resources to COVID-19 infections from other life-threatening diseases; food deprivation; neglect of or difficulty in seeking treatment for existing ailments; and fatal medical conditions and suicides triggered by stress and depression. In India we must add the deaths of migrants walking or cycling several hundred kilometres, or travelling on trains organized belatedly by the government but without food and water.

Unfortunately, reliable data about deaths with reasons are not available in India especially in real time. But we may reasonably expect non-COVID deaths in India to be even more than the European countries studied by the *Financial Times*, because of mass hunger, high inequality, high levels of abject poverty, weak social security arrangements, and a broken public health system. Also, as we shall see, in the race to be prepare for the pandemic, and for fear of health workers or non-COVID patients contracting the infection, the non-COVID health systems were substantially shut down with the lockdown.

In a discussion organized by the Centre for Equity Studies, Vandana Prasad, a noted practitioner of community public-health, said the government transposed a public health problem into a policing and law and order problem. 'What we have done,' she said, 'is bad public health, and it is critical from our understanding that we frame it in that way. Lockdown is not simply disastrous economics. We should not be tempted into thinking of the food and job crises only as collateral damage. To not think of social determinants of health is bad public health. Hunger and livelihoods are an essential part of public health.' She also said that the data about possible spikes in deaths from TB, childbirth complications and hunger-related causes should also be shared to have a fuller idea about the impact of the lockdown. A report from Oxfam titled 'The Hunger Virus' estimates that 122 million (12.2 crore) people will be pushed into starvation due to the lockdown, and more people will die of lockdown-induced hunger than from COVID-19 infection.[138]

In the same discussion, Vikram Patel, Harvard-based public health psychiatrist, agreed that no epidemic is only a bio-medical phenomenon. It is also very importantly a social phenomenon. Social scientists too should have advised the government and not just health professionals. The outcomes of mass hunger are tragic, Patel explained, because the lockdown has turned the country back years, even decades. Likewise, Keshav Desiraju, former Health Secretary of India, spoke of people with other illnesses being very badly hit, by what they have lost in terms of care because of the lockdown: those not getting diabetes medication, TB treatment, and other essential care. And of course, unorganised labour, without jobs or daily income. The impact of job losses on food deprivation among unorganised labour now without daily income would be very high. The job losses would also affect their mental health and well-being. Reports of increased attempted suicides, domestic violence and unwanted pregnancies should also alert us to what the lockdown has done to their lives.

A July UNICEF report[139] stated that the significant additional pressure on already overburdened social and health service delivery systems threatened to reverse decades of development gains for children. There were significant disruptions in essential health and nutrition services, including immunization, growth monitoring, and ante-natal and post-natal care for pregnant women. These disruptions in services have continued even after the lockdown because of closure of health facilities, lack of adequate health care workers and sometimes irrational fear, triggered by sensationalist official messaging, of infection at health centres. The report estimated that between July and the end of 2020, up to 6,000 children could die every day across the world from preventable illnesses due to both direct and indirect COVID-19-related disruptions in essential services. Eighty million children may be at risk of diphtheria, measles and polio due to disruptions in supply chains and immunization services. With the closure of schools, 369 million children missed out on school meals, and many of these children rely on these meals as a source of daily nutrition. Every third malnourished child on the planet is Indian, and every third Indian child is malnourished. By the end of the year, chances are that their numbers would grow further.

Even seven months into the lockdown, Radhika Bordia observed that when the Delhi government thought it fit to reopen malls, gyms and pubs, it still did not open up the preschool *anganwadi* feeding centres, which for decades have been India's principal defence against the malnourishment of its young children. Delhi was not alone: in fact, Chhattisgarh was the only state government which had prioritized the reopening of these centres, where children are not only fed but their weights monitored to ensure that severe malnutrition is identified early and treated before it takes too high a toll on the child's health and survival. 'Severe malnourishment, wasting, is an acute situation with a close relationship with mortality, and six months is a long time for an essential service like an *anganwadi* to be shut,' said Vandana Prasad, public health paediatrician. 'This is going to have long-term consequences on mortalities, morbidities and malnutrition.'[140]

There was an official or unofficial suspension of OPD and other services in most public and private hospitals. Even premier public hospitals, like AIIMS and Safdarjung in Delhi, suspended registering new patients in their OPDs from the beginning of lockdown for a month and a half. There are numerous reports of private hospitals either formally closing down or refusing to treat patients, both for COVID-19 and other ailments. A 65-year-old man in kidney failure needed dialysis twice a week. Private hospitals which had administered his dialysis before the lockdown now refused unless he presented a negative COVID-19 report. They said they would not admit patients without such certification. Getting tested for COVID-19 was not only expensive, but till late 2020 Delhi government guidelines also barred testing for people who did not show symptoms. In desperation, the ailing man went to the emergency department of Dr Ram Manohar Lohia Hospital, a prominent public hospital in the national capital, which, fortunately, did not turn him away. Likewise, a 31-year-old pregnant woman travelled from Loni in Uttar Pradesh on 3rd May for medical attention to a hospital near Delhi's Jama Masjid. She was in pain and complained of blood spotting. 'All her check-ups during the pregnancy had happened at that hospital, so we wanted to take her there despite the lockdown. However, when we reached Delhi, doctors told us that some people in the hospital had tested positive for COVID-19 and they could not admit her,' said her husband.[141] In Mumbai, too, medical treatment was denied often to pregnant women. A senior health official admitted that 'the administration is struggling to address the issue of pregnant women, who are either turned away by private hospitals or are asked to seek admission at state-run facilities'. Almost all civic and state-run hospitals in Mumbai reported a rise in the number of deliveries because private hospitals were turning women away.[142] Similar stories came in from Bangalore[143] and indeed most other parts of the country.

Patients suffering from diseases other than COVID-19 were neglected, excluded, even left to die as hospitals scrambled to make beds available for the current or future load of COVID-19 patients. Doctors say patients coming for other ailments, including heart disease, strokes and cancer, fell dramatically. People with symptoms also avoided hospitals, fearful of catching COVID-19 in the crowds there or not being attended to by hospital staff. The entire medical system shifted focus so overwhelmingly to COVID-19 that other diseases were almost forgotten. All 'non-essential surgeries' were halted, and most ICU beds reserved for COVID-19. This attempt to check COVID-19 unwittingly increased deaths, possibly massively, from other causes.

Meanwhile, public health services in every other sector took a severe beating. Across India, data from National Health Mission shows—as the UNICEF Report had predicted—that there was 'a 69% reduction in measles, mumps and rubella vaccination in children, a 21% reduction in institutional deliveries, a 50% reduction in clinic attendance for acute cardiac events and, surprisingly, a 32% fall in inpatient care for pulmonary conditions in March 2020, compared with March 2019'.[144] All of this would have taken a severe toll of life and health.

Dr Shah Alam Khan, a dedicated and compassionate paediatric cancer surgeon at the AIIMS hospital in Delhi has often spoken and written movingly of 'the cancer refugees'—

poor families who shift to Delhi for the cure of their children and other members with cancer for the years of their treatment. They live on the pavements outside the hospital because they cannot afford to rent a room, and survive by casual labour. He told me that two days into the lockdown, they had all been swept off the streets. Where they had gone, he did not know, but the lockdown had cruelly extinguished all chances of their care and cure.

The World Health Organisation estimates that India has 15 million malaria cases causing 20,000 deaths per year. The lockdown has disrupted preventive anti-malaria programmes in most states.[145] The thousand-odd deaths caused by COVID-19 in the two months of lockdown, tragic as all deaths, still look trivial compared with the mass deaths caused by other diseases getting low priority. In India Ischemic heart diseases alone kill 4000 people per day.[146] Nearly 2000 die every day of diarrhoea, and over 1200 of TB.

India has 25 million cases of TB. Current models of untreated tuberculosis have found fatality in around 70% for smear-positive tuberculosis.[147] The impact of the lockdown on TB diagnosis, reporting and access to drugs is particularly distressing, because TB burdens the poor a lot more, and untreated TB leads to death in 50 to 70 percent cases,[148] whereas untreated COVID is likely to endanger at the most 20% people who require oxygen, and even within these 5% seriously, who would require ICU hospitalization and ventilator support. A study and modelling done by the Stop TB Partnership show that lockdowns across countries, and especially in India, led to curtailed diagnosis and notifications (a way of documenting incidence and prevalence of cases) and availability of TB drugs.[149] This is supplemented by

WHO consolidated data from India's reporting, showing that weekly counts of reported cases dropped by 75% in the three weeks following 22 March. It is important to underline again that undiagnosed and untreated TB is far more likely to result in death. By contrast, untreated COVID-19 in India has a mortality rate of around just 2.5%. In simple words, if a people with TB are denied treatment (as has happened because of the lockdown and continuing disruptions caused by diverting most public health resources to COVID-19) five to seven out of ten will die. But from COVID-19, one in 20, and more likely one in 40 of those infected will die. It is bizarre, then, to observe scarce resources being diverted from the prevention, detection and treatment of TB to the present emperor of maladies, COVID-19.

We have seen in India the perilous reassignment of health personnel, testing equipment and beds, and a reduction in TB testing and detection. My colleagues work with homeless people with TB in Delhi, and we have observed that DOTS (Directly Observed Treatment-Short-Course) centres in Delhi have been either closed or are only dealing with existing patients, not new cases. Health personnel and diagnostic kits designated to deal with TB patients are co-opted to deal with COVID-19 patients and diagnostics. Moreover, nutrition is vital to TB care, and due to the disruption in work and income, it is becoming harder for the most vulnerable persons to access basic nutritious food. TB patients are immunocompromised and at greater risk of developing severe symptoms in case they catch the COVID-19 infection.

The same downward cascade impact can be seen on reproductive and maternal health. The Foundation for Reproductive Health Services (FRHS) fears a rise in unwanted pregnancies and unsafe abortions because of closed access to reproductive health services, contraception and family planning services. Family planning services such as Sterilization and Intra-Uterine Contraceptive Devices (IUCD) were shut down from mid-March till further notice. The FRHS predicts 1.94 million unwanted pregnancies and 1.45 million abortions, including 834,042 unsafe abortions, in 2020.[150]

Official health data which is pouring in is alarming. There were over 580,000 fewer institutional deliveries in April than in January, which could indicate that many more women had potentially unsafe deliveries at home. The number of children who got the Bacille Calmette-Guérin (BCG) vaccine—which prevents severe tuberculosis—in April was half that of the number for January. National Health Mission data shows that outpatient attendance in April fell to half its January levels, with 6.9 crore, or 69 million, fewer outpatient visits. This included outpatient treatment for serious conditions including cancer and acute heart disease. There was a 45% fall in the number of patients registered for TB treatment and a 60% fall in men screened for HIV in June 2020. The number of surgeries, both major and minor, also fell by over half in June as compared to January. Doctors fear 'a coming storm'; that patients will end up with more dangerous and unmanaged forms of the diseases they were suffering from.[151]

The lockdown also led to a shadow mental health crisis which will continue long after it was lifted. The Indian Psychiatry Society (IPS) found a sharp increase in mental illness cases after the lockdown. There was a 20% rise in cases, with at least one in five Indians suffering from mental health distress. Given the stigma associated with mental illness, the numbers are likely to be much higher. The loss of employment, wages, businesses during the lockdown and the fear of not finding jobs in the future increased the distress.[152] The grim prognosis of the IPS is that 'India will suffer from a massive health crisis due to unemployment, alcohol abuse, economic hardship, domestic violence and indebtedness. While this will affect most of the population, it will disproportionately affect the poor, most vulnerable and marginalised groups.' These are also the groups that have the least access to professional psychiatric care.

The National Commission of Women (NCW) estimated in mid-April an almost 100% increase in domestic violence during the lockdown.[153] Journalists and feminist researchers found many instances of women who were locked in with abusive partners—and these were only a small number of such cases that ever got reported. For many women, the loss of income due to the lockdown translated to a loss of bargaining power in the household and disempowerment in their relationships. My colleagues met Madhu, a sex worker, who spoke about her friend's predicament. She was beaten by her husband almost every night during the lockdown. 'Late at night when she is sleeping, around 2 a.m., he will wake her up and beat her. He tells her, "Bring me money." She is stuck there…You tell me, when everything is closed, from factories to shops, how will the poor woman alone bring him anything?'

Feelings of despair and helplessness, anxiety and loneliness have been aggravated by the stigma and fear created at least in part by official messaging about COVID-19 and the policing of victims. People infected by the virus are treated as though they are criminals, with police sealing their homes.

Incarceration, forced isolation and the hardship and rigours inflicted on those who are made to quarantine only make things worse.[154]

One of the inadvertent outcomes of the lockdown was also the closing down of rehabilitation centres for the patients of substance abuse, and then the problems in accessing counselling sessions online.[155] It affected in particular adolescent youth, and deprived them of the opportunity to seek therapy away from the confines of their home.

There was also the intense loneliness of grief as people lost loved ones to the COVID-19 virus at the peak of the lockdown and there was no support—not from the state, and often not even from friends and relatives. There are many tragic stories told about this. One that I will never forget is of the mother and daughter of a retired policeman who had died of COVID-19 struggling to claim his body from a government hospital in Delhi, and bury him. They had been in quarantine for ten days when the daughter received the call informing her of her father's death. The local police gave them permission to leave home, but the relatives they called up to help them claim the body from the hospital refused. Their neighbours shunned them, and when they called their parish priest, he said he would pray for their soul but would not come to be with them or conduct the funeral prayers. An acquaintance, a nurse, came to help them complete the paperwork at the hospital, which took till early evening, by which time the hospital had no staff to spare who could accompany the body to the cemetery. They were told they would have to manage on their own somehow. The Ola driver who drove them to the hospital refused to take them to the burial ground. Desperate, they reached out to an auto-rickshaw driver, Hussain, whom they sometimes employed. 'The mother and daughter were in pain and I couldn't refuse them,' he said. 'They were alone on the saddest day of their lives. No relatives, no preachers they believed in turned up. I couldn't let down the humanity in me at such an hour.' Sanjay, a helper at the cemetery, dug the 14-foot grave required for victims of the Coronavirus. 'Whether a COVID death or any other kind of death, this is my job and I wouldn't pull back because of fear or stigma,' he said later. A pastor who happened to be passing by noticed there was a burial taking place without a priest and stopped and read a passage from the Bible to console the mother and daughter. The daughter recalled later, 'My father's coffin was buried by a Muslim auto driver, a Hindu cemetery helper and two other God-sent angels, who proved that humanity is greater than any religion or belief we blindly put our faith [in]...My father will take the heavenly abode, but I am not sure about people who denied help because they were afraid.'[156]

*

The human, social and political consequences of the lockdown will probably outlast even the economic and health consequences. UNICEF and ILO fear a rise in child labour in India, because as families struggle with job loss and hunger, children will be pressed into unsafe and exploitative work. There is also evidence of an increase in trafficking for commercial sex and cheap labour.[157] A study by the *Indian Express* in October 2020, almost five months after the lockdown was lifted, found that with schools shut and families in dire economic distress, children in much larger numbers than in normal times were being pushed into child labour, brothels, sweatshops and early marriages. These tragedies are expected to grow and intensify further as the economy tries to 'recover', because labour contractors will be on the prowl in search of cheap labour, and children are both cheap and submissive. Childline, which works with governments to respond to complaints of child trafficking and abuse, received nearly 30 lakh calls during the lockdown. It also recorded 10,000 early child marriages during the period. One headmaster in 24 Parganas in Bengal set up his own informal helpline and rescue mission for girls who were being forced into marriages.[158]

The schooling of a child in a poor family may be interrupted because the child does not have the hardware, connectivity and uninterrupted electricity to enable online learning, and may drop out of education completely, assisting the family instead in its economic and health challenges. Many respondents in a survey conducted by the Centre for Equity Studies and the Delhi Research Group spoke of the unlikelihood of their return to education after the rupture caused by the lockdown, more so of girls and children with disability. Masses of first-generation learners are likely to find their education terminated permanently.

Above all, the lockdown has resulted in a complete breakdown of the trust of the working poor in every institution of the republic. Every single institution failed the labouring poor when they most needed it. The wounds caused by the collapse of hope and faith will be the hardest to heal.

9

Did the Coronavirus Turn Muslim?

The pandemic, made worse by severe lockdowns, has been a time of immense dislocation and dread for all Indians. But as it unfolded, it became a time of particular despair and desolation if you were an Indian Muslim.

The years since the Narendra Modi-led BJP was voted to power have been marked by Muslim baiting almost as policy, which has resulted in unrelenting anti-Muslim hatred—in everyday interactions across much of the country, in large sections of the media and on social media, and among members of the government. There have been unimaginably brutal, videotaped lynchings, even as there has been a systematic and near-complete expulsion of Muslims from electoral politics. And in December 2019 the Modi government used its brute strength in the Lok Sabha to push through the Citizenship (Amendment) Act (CAA), which makes religion a consideration for granting Indian citizenship for the first time, and singles out Muslim residents in particular. Coupled with the proposed National Register of Citizens (NRC)—a connection that the Home Minister Amit Shah himself has made repeatedly—this would give the government the power to take away citizenship rights of Indian Muslims at will, keeping them in constant dread and insecurity.

Immediately after the CAA was passed, millions of India's Muslims, supported by large numbers of secular non-Muslims, began a countrywide resistance. It grew into one of the biggest and most incandescent democratic movements since Independence. Members and supporters of the government unleashed a campaign of vicious propaganda, hate-speech and intimidation against the protestors, and immediately following a series of open threats and calls for violence by senior members of the BJP, the national capital was rocked by communal violence in the last week of February 2020. Fifty-three people were killed in Muslim-majority areas of North East Delhi; nearly 500 people were injured and many more displaced; hundreds of homes and shops were looted and burnt down and 17 mosques desecrated and damaged. The violence was allowed to continue for five days, with the police either refusing to act or being openly partisan.

The first cases of COVID-19 infection were being detected in India around this time and it was clear that the pandemic had reached our door—less than a month later, Prime Minister Modi was to announce his nationwide lockdown. We could have expected that the demons of hate and bigotry—which had resulted in such savagery and devastation just days before—would be at least temporarily exiled and the country would come together to unitedly fight the terrifying pandemic and the mass hunger and unemployment caused by the lockdown. But the ruling establishment had other plans.

From March 13 to 15, an orthodox Muslim reform group called the Tablighi Jamaat held a large international gathering in their centre, or markaz, in Delhi's West Nizamuddin locality, with participants from different parts of India and also from Malaysia, Indonesia, Thailand, Bangladesh and other countries. The meeting was held after securing due permissions from the government. From the early days of the shock lockdown, people across the country were glued to their televisions and smartphones for news of the virus and its spread. The official briefings quickly shifted to depicting the Tablighi gathering as the epicentre and central cause of the infection in India. On 1st April, with no evidence, no figures to support the claim, the Union Health Ministry explicitly blamed the Tablighi Jamaat for the spike in COVID-19 cases in the country: 'Till now, there are 1637 COVID-19 cases, including 386 new positive cases and three new deaths since yesterday. The main reason for [the] increased number of cases is that members of the Tablighi Jamaat have travelled across the country,' said Lav Agarwal, Joint Secretary and spokesperson of the Health Ministry.[159] Four days later, the spokesperson made an even more egregious, entirely speculative statement: 'The doubling rate [of COVID-19 infection] in India is 4.1 days. Had the congregation at Nizamuddin not happened and additional cases not come, this would have been about 7.14 days.'[160] It was not only the union government that was responsible for spreading this canard. The Delhi government in its briefings, for instance, routinely used the term 'Markaz Masjid cases'.[161]

There were obvious statistical biases in all of this, as pointed out by Shoaib Daniyal in *Scroll*, because whereas (at a time when testing was very low) more than 25,000 Jamaat members and their contacts were aggressively traced and tested, the participants in other large religious and political gatherings held around the same time, including those patronised and attended by senior leaders of the BJP like the chief minister of Uttar Pradesh, were not actively pursued or tested to even a fraction of the degree to which the Tablighi participants were. Statisticians explain that if during those days of reporting the majority of cases which were tested were from the Tablighi Jamaat, then it is not surprising that the majority of identified COVID-19 cases would also be linked to the gathering.[162]

The Jamaat meeting was indeed injudicious and would ultimately cost many lives; it should have been cancelled by the organisers when evidence of a global pandemic was clear. However, to place the matter in perspective, such irresponsibility, or such tendency to misjudge the seriousness of the medical emergency, was rampant at that time. Even as late as 13 March, the central government itself publicly maintained that there was no health emergency in India. Parliament was in session through all of this period, and as late as 18 March the President was hosting a breakfast for several Members of Parliament where no rules of distancing were observed (there was even a group photo session).[163] Religious, political and social gatherings were held during this period at many other places—from the ISKCON Temple in Ahmedabad to the Raj Bhavan in Bhopal—but these hardly attracted attention from the media or in official briefings. One among these was a gathering of 3,500 Sikh pilgrims in Nanded in Maharashtra, which led to a spike in infections in Punjab when they returned. But Sikhs were never demonized for this. Violations continued even *after* the lockdown. Amid chants of 'Jai Sri Ram', hundreds of devotees assembled in temples in various parts of West Bengal on the occasion of

Ram Navami on 2nd April .[164] Again, violating the lockdown orders, hundreds of people joined in the Siddhalingeswara temple chariot festival in Chitapur village in Kalburgi area of Karnataka on 16th April.[165]

The flames of hate against Muslims lit by the tenor of official briefings, amplified by hysterical media reports and biased television debates, then engulfed the entire country, their spread aided by the loyal trolls of social media, including members of the infamous BJP IT Cell. A flood of fake videos was unleashed on the internet, depicting Muslims deliberately smearing vegetables and fruits with their saliva, spitting into food served in restaurants and coughing into the faces of other people, all with the intent of infecting non-Muslims.[166] Hashtags like #CoronaJihad, #BioJihad and #TablighiJamaatVirus began to circulate and trend.[167]

Two researchers, Soundarya Iyer of the French Institute of Pondicherry and Shoibal Chakravarty of the Divecha Centre for Climate Change at the Indian Institute of Science found 11,074 stories published from 271 media sources with the term 'Tablighi Jamaat' from 20 March to 20 April. Their analysis noted that the words that frequently appeared alongside 'Tablighi' and 'Jamaat' were 'coronavirus', 'Delhi', 'lockdown', 'violating', 'crime', 'spitting', 'terrorist' and 'jihad'. Even a leading newspaper like the *Times of India*, the country's largest selling English daily, carried as many as 1863 stories of the Tablighi Jamaat in these five weeks, which were shared 3,19, 921 times on Facebook. 'These stories fed into an epidemic of Islamophobic fake news and hate speech,' they wrote in *The Hindu BusinessLine*. This was 'exploited for the production of misinformation and hate speech.'[168]

Their study only covered the print media. Television

channels were even more shrill. ABP Live described members of the Jamaat as '*manav bomb*'[169] or human bomb, while Sudhir Chaudhary of Zee News said that the 'Tablighi Jamaat betrayed the nation'.[170] Political leaders of the BJP were only too willing to amplify further this feverish hate mongering. Former Maharashtra chief minister Devendra Fadnavis, for instance, also described the Jamaat members as '*manav bomb*'.[171]

The consequences were immediate, and in some cases, deadly. The members of the Tablighi Jamaat were of course the most directly stigmatised and hated among non-Muslims across the country, on par with terrorists, but all other Muslims, especially the poor, also suffered. Dilshad Mohammad, a 38-year-old singer and shopkeeper in Himachal Pradesh's Una district was taken to a regional hospital by the police to be tested for the Coronavirus because he had come in contact with two people who had attended the Tablighi gathering in Delhi. He tested negative for COVID-19 and was sent back home, but he could not handle the taunts and boycott of his neighbours and slit his wrists before hanging himself in his home on 5 April. He left behind a note that said, 'I am not anyone's enemy.' Days later, a 30-year old Assamese man who had attended the Jamaat gathering slit his throat after he tested positive for the viral infection in a hospital in Akola in Maharashtra.

My colleagues and I heard numerous reports, on our helplines and during our food distribution drives, of physical attacks on Muslims, both members of the Tablighi Jamaat and others. Muslim truck drivers were beaten up in Arunachal Pradesh. Unknown men fired at a mosque in Dhankot village in Haryana. Two vegetable vendors in UP's Mahoba district were roughed up and prevented from selling vegetables by people who accused them of being 'Tablighis' and spreading the Coronavirus. Muslim fruit-sellers were similarly roughed up in Haldwani in Uttarakhand. Nine migrant Kashmiri labourers were thrashed with cricket bats in Barot, Himachal Pradesh, and left with broken bones; the sarpanch and other residents of the village admitted that TV reports and WhatsApp messages had 'poisoned the minds of people'.[172] In Assam, a murderous mob surrounded daily-wage workers who were digging a pond, suspecting them of being members of the Tablighi Jamaat. In Bengaluru, a Mulsim woman and her son who were distributing food to slum-dwellers were assaulted by men armed with cricket bats—'Why must you do this in a Hindu area?' the men asked, accusing them of being 'terrorists from Nizamuddin'.[173] Some of my Muslim colleagues who volunteered for Karwan-e-Mohabbat's countrywide feeding campaign reported that they were brusquely turned away from Hindu settlements even when they went there to distribute much needed dry rations. Zafarul Islam, the chairperson of the Delhi Minorities Commission, reported that 200 men attacked and ransacked a mosque in Mukhmelpur village in North West Delhi.[174] A mob kicked and humiliated Muslims fishing in the Krishna river near Bidari village in Karnataka's Bagalkot district—in the video of the attack, they are heard shouting, 'You people [Muslims] are the ones spreading this disease.' In another village in the same district, men attacked people praying in a mosque.[175]

The list is a long one. It should be recalled that all of this was happening during the severest phase of the nationwide lockdown, and at a time when the prime minister was instructing people to act as one and bang thalis and switch off all lights across the country in order to strengthen the fight against the virus. The PM, of course, made no appeal during his televised national addresses for people to stop the hate-mongering and the hate crimes. He did not even acknowledge that such ugliness was about. It was only on 19 April, three weeks after the vicious propaganda against Muslims began, that a responsible-sounding tweet went out from the prime minister's official handle. Even here the beasts of bigotry and hate were not named; only a vague platitude was delivered. The online magazine *Article 14* gave details of the message and its timing:

> On 19 April 2020, Prime Minister Narendra Modi spoke up for the first time. He tweeted: '#COVID19 does not see race, religion, colour, caste, creed, language or borders before striking. Our response and conduct thereafter should attach primacy to unity and brotherhood. We are in this together.'
>
> The tweet came within an hour of a body representing an organisation of Islamic nations, many of them India's strategic partners, criticised the 'unrelenting vicious #Islamophobic campaign in #India maligning Muslims for spread of #COVID-19 as well as their negative profiling in media subjecting them to discrimination & violence with impunity'.[176]

Not surprisingly, the tweet made little impact, if any at all. The targeting of Muslims continued.

Along with the physical attacks and intimidation, there were widespread calls for the social and economic boycott of all Muslim vendors and workers. Many videos surfaced of Muslim vegetable sellers being driven away or even beaten when their identity was known; of one Muslim vegetable seller being caught because he said his name was Sanjay and not Javed; and of Hindu vegetable sellers placing saffron flags on their wooden carts so that they could be identified as Hindu and, therefore, 'safe'.[177] Muslim agricultural workers in Western Uttar Pradesh were asked to get themselves tested for COVID before they returned to their fields.[178] Some of these boycott calls turned violent. According to a detailed report in *The* Wire, Gujjar Muslim milk-sellers in Punjab's Hoshiarpur district were beaten up in Hindu-majority villages and forced to pour vast quantities of milk into a riverbed.[179] Through the lockdown and even after, they were prohibited from selling milk in many districts of Punjab, allegedly with the support of the district heads. Three months after the lockdown was announced, they were still not being allowed to graze their cattle in the village. 'Earlier our cattle used to graze on grass or crop leftovers in the vacant fields. Now, we are short of fodder and dry chaff for them. Even now that the lockdown is over, our entry is still banned,' pastoralist Sher Ali told *The Wire*. 'The panchayat and villagers even stopped the local vegetable vendor from coming to our houses. They told him that we were spreading Coronavirus and he should desist from visiting us.'[180]

Posters with similar calls to keep all Muslims away came up in many states, including Assam and Karnataka—openly calling for a complete boycott of Muslims, even barring their entry into villages.[181] Here again, the list is a long one.

The malign official targeting of the followers of the Tablighi Jamaat did not end. Both Indian and foreign members were kept in quarantine for nearly four times the mandatory period of 14 days, even though they tested negative, sometimes twice or even thrice. They were not allowed to meet their families, and spent the month of Ramzan fasting in detention without the religiously mandated sehri and iftar meals. They spent a lonely, dark Eid. In many districts of Uttar Pradesh, 2,727 Jamaat members were detained in extended quarantine in this way.[182] *Newsclick* spoke to the District Magistrate of one such district, Barabanki, in which Tablighi members were being held in what could only be described as illegal detention. Adarsh Singh, the District Magistrate, refused to comment on why Tablighi Jamaat members were being kept in quarantine for such a long period even after testing negative. He said he was just following government directives.[183]

*

On 2 April, the union Home Ministry identified 960 foreigners who had attended the Nizamuddin congregation and blacklisted them. It charged them with visa violations under the Foreigners Act, 1946—entering India on a tourist visa and indulging in missionary activities—as also violations of the Disaster Management Act 2005 and the Epidemic Diseases Act 1897. The men were imprisoned, and numerous other sections of the Indian law were heaped upon them, including 'disobedience to order duly promulgated by public servant' (section 188), 'negligent act' likely to spread infectious disease (section 269), 'malignant act' likely to spread infectious disease (section 270), and 'public nuisance' (section 290). [184]

It took two judges with a conscience to finally bring the persecution of at least some of these men to an end, and to sharply call out the motives of the government. The two judges of the Bombay High Court, while quashing three

FIRs against 35 petitioners—29 of them foreign nationals—decried what they described as the 'big propaganda' in the print and electronic media against the pilgrims which blamed them for spreading COVID-19. The judgement did not flinch from identifying the political objectives of the action against the members of the Jamaat. 'A political government tries to find scapegoat[s] when there is pandemic or calamity and the circumstances show that there is a probability that these foreigners were chosen to make them scapegoats,' the court said. 'The aforesaid circumstances and the latest figures of infection in India show that such action against present petitioners should not have been taken.'

The judgment also underlined the duties of the government towards both displaying compassion and promoting fraternity. 'During the situation created by [the] COVID-19 pandemic, we need to show more tolerance and we need to be more sensitive towards our guests, particularly like the present petitioners,' Justice T.V. Nalawade declared in the judgement. 'The allegations made show that instead of helping them, we lodged them in jails by making allegations that they are responsible for violation of travel documents, they are responsible for spreading of virus, etc.' The judges also recalled the message of Swami Vivekanand in his historic 1893 speech at the World's Parliament of Religions in Chicago. 'He had started his speech with words like "sisters and brothers", showing that he believed in universal brotherhood. He believed that all religions are true,' the judges said, and reminded the executive that the world 'fraternity' was an integral part of India's Constitution.

The judges also rejected the confidential reports of the union home ministry that charged the Tablighis with violating the terms of their tourist visa by 'spreading Muslim religion by giving speeches in Masjid'. The judges maintained that visa rules do not prohibit foreigners from visiting religious places and holding religious discourses.

*

We all know that the COVID-19 pandemic is caused by a highly contagious and potentially deadly mutating virus. But for this to mutate in India, within a few days of a national lockdown, into a 'conspiracy' by Muslims to infect and kill non-Muslims is a stunning accomplishment of right-wing communication and mobilisation with few parallels anywhere in the modern world. I spoke to many working-class Hindus who are not normally Islamophobic. Almost every one of them was convinced that the spread of the virus was mainly caused by Indian Muslims. They had been persuaded that Muslims were spreading the virus either because their religious bigotry led them to continue stubbornly gathering in large groups for worship and endangering everyone; or, much worse, that they actually chose to infect non-Muslims in order to eliminate them and establish Islamic rule in India.

It is hard to believe that the language and tenor of official briefings which succeeded in making the Tablighi Jamaat, and through them the entire Muslim community, centrally culpable for the spread of the killer virus was accidental. The head of the BJP's IT Cell, Amit Malviya, had tweeted on 1st April: 'Last 3 months have seen an Islamic insurrection of sorts, first in the name of anti-CAA protests from Shaheen Bagh to Jamia, Jafrabad to Seelampur. And now the illegal gathering of the radical Tablighi Jamaat at the markaz. It needs a fix!' A union minister, Mukhtar Abbas Naqvi (ironically, responsible for minorities' welfare), also of the BJP, went so far as to describe the Tablighi gathering as a 'Talibani crime'.[185]

Until then, the dominant heart-breaking images of the lockdown which had pierced public consciousness were of the lakhs of desperate migrants walking on the highways. Uncomfortable questions were being raised about why the Union government had not used the preceding many weeks to greatly ramp up the production of medical equipment and testing kits, and why it had not imposed restrictions on large gatherings much earlier.

But now, supported by those large sections of the television and print media which had been Islamophobic even in normal times, a narrative that the COVID-19 virus had spread in India because of religiously bigoted and socially irresponsible Muslims was manufactured and propagated across the country with astonishing speed and efficiency.

Ordinary Hindus may not be communal. But it is extraordinary how easy it is to influence them with highly charged communal propaganda.

In coping both with the fears of the pandemic and the devastating human costs which the lockdown has extracted, Indian Muslims have suffered as much as their sisters and brothers of other faiths. In fact, more than any other socio-religious community, urban Muslims are self-employed in petty businesses and were therefore more vulnerable, because they were not registered as workers and so not eligible for even the paltry financial aid extended by the Indian state to registered workers.[186] Yet, while other Indians were battling fear, loss, dislocation, joblessness, hunger and a frightening epidemic which no government in the world seemed able to vanquish, Indian Muslims had been forced to battle not only all of these, but also the extreme and utterly irrational hatred of their neighbours.[187]

Elsewhere in the world as well, the fear of the virus spurred hate and a similar quest for scapegoats, such as against the Roma in Eastern Europe, and against Chinese people outside China. This led Yuval Noah Harari, the famed Israeli intellectual and historian, to remark, 'Humanity has all the scientific knowledge and technological tools to overcome the virus. The really big problem is our inner demons, our own hatred, greed and ignorance. I'm afraid that people are reacting to this crisis not with global solidarity but with hatred, blaming other countries, blaming ethnic and religious minorities.'[188] In India, an enormously diverse country, but with a ruling dispensation committed to an ideology of religious supremacism and majoritarian rule, the problem attained even greater and more dangerous proportions.

In this climate of hate, there were a few rays of hope. Most remarkably, simple kindness and humanity, however rare; and the ability to find reasons for love and forgiveness even in the midst of great persecution and injustice. Priya Ramani writes of a 31-year-old member of the Tablighi Jamaat from Djibouti, Gulel Abdi Ilahi, who was released because of the Bombay High Court order after spending 60 nightmarish days in a prison cell in Ahmednagar. 'We are not criminals but were treated as criminals,' he told Ramani. 'I had never been even near a jail in my entire life before this.' There were sometimes 25 people, including many criminals, sharing his cell. There was little place to sleep, one common toilet, and you had to bathe in front of other people. But he remembers his kind Hindu jailor, who gave him dates, water and fruit to break his fast each evening during Ramzan. 'He respected me.' Ilahi said. 'He was a good man. He would speak to us, say you are not alone, everything will be good.' Because of men like him, Gulel Abdi Ilahi says, despite everything, he still loves India.[189]

*

The lockdown was a double catastrophe for the survivors of the communal violence in North-East Delhi. Exactly a month before the nationwide lockdown, this largest district in the national capital burned in the most horrific Hindu-Muslim violence since Partition. It left at least 53 people dead, hundreds injured, and several hundred homes and shops burned and looted. The union government, unsurprisingly, did nothing. And the Delhi government did little to help the hundreds who had become homeless, apart from reluctantly setting up a few basic relief camps. It was social workers, peace workers, lawyers and compassionate ordinary citizens who tried to fill the gap by providing some meaningful assistance.

But even this assistance and the haphazardly run camps were shut down because of the lockdown. My colleagues Meera and Varna, who were among the many young volunteers of Karwan-e-Mohabbat working with the survivors of the violence, recall how a camp at Eidgah was closed overnight—most families were given a token sum of 3000 rupees, some ration which would barely last two days and asked to fend for themselves. One of the residents in the camp recalled that this was one of the most traumatic nights of his life. He said, 'I did not know where to go. It was raining heavily and I was homeless with my two little children. We had nowhere to go!' Over the period of the lockdown, families affected by the riots were displaced from their homes not once, but multiple times. They had to hunt for shelter in their relatives' homes, and in some cases even strangers' homes. Many did not have the money for rent and were facing evictions. The anxiety amongst the families who were without a house peaked during this time. The volunteers who could help them were locked down. Livelihoods destroyed by the riot had stayed so, with no scope for recovery. Food insecurity had increased and spread further to even those who were not displaced in the riot. Health facilities had become even more inaccessible.[190]

Meanwhile, in the dark shadow of the lockdown, the Delhi police—controlled by the union government of India—was busy with tasks entirely unrelated to controlling the COVID-19 pandemic. The demanding schedule of the police force through these weeks was instead packed with searching homes and offices, confiscating phones and documents, and questioning, detaining, arresting and sending to prison large numbers of people who had participated in the anti-CAA protests in Shaheen Bagh, Jamia, Jafrabad and other parts of the city. The charges levelled against the women and men picked up by the Delhi police related firstly to their alleged 'seditious' and 'communal' role in organizing protests against the discriminatory CAA and NRC. They were further accused of instigating and participating in the communal carnage which had engulfed working class settlements in north-east Delhi. It is instructive that these arrests were being mounted at a time when the Supreme Court had directed governments to decongest jails to prevent the spread of the Coronavirus.[191]

It is also revealing that while the police redoubled its

detentions and arrests after a brief respite following the imposition of the lockdown, legal services were not included in 'essential services' permitted to operate during the lockdown. This meant, in effect, the suspension of the fundamental rights of accused persons; they could not be represented by their lawyers while they were in the custody of the police or in courts. The accused persons were presented by the police before magistrates, often inside jail premises, with no lawyers allowed to defend them, or in the lower courts which have no facilities for video-hearings.[192] It was as though during what is a health emergency, the principles of rule of law and equal protection of the law were also under lockdown.

Journalists, lawyers and human rights defenders had little access to those being targeted by these concerted police operations. The exact numbers of detentions and arrests were therefore hard to confirm in the undeclared emergency that had been imposed in the country. A few reports of a surge in such arrests, almost entirely of Muslim residents, in North East Delhi still came in. Deploring these 'random arrests' the Delhi Minorities Commission sent a notice to the Delhi Police Commissioner, stating that the police was 'arresting young Muslim boys by their dozens every single day' even during the lockdown.[193] *The Hindu* reported that from 22 March to mid-April, roughly the first month of the lockdown, around 25-30 arrests were made from the violence affected areas of North-East Delhi.[194] *The Indian Express* reported a total of 802 arrests had been made in relation to the Delhi riots by the police, of which at least 50 were made during the lockdown.[195] Some other reports, in news sites like the *Quint*, put the figure much higher—that six to seven arrests were being made every day in the Muslim-majority areas of North-East Delhi.[196] This last estimate was also ratified by my lawyer colleagues who worked closely with local residents in the weeks after the carnage. This spike in detention and arrests had come reportedly after the Union Home Ministry's instructions to the crime branch of the Delhi Police at the end of March.[197]

These arrests were—and continue to be, even as this book is being written—characterised by an utter disregard for legal norms. The families of those who were rounded up were not even given copies of the FIRs. The psychological and emotional toll on the families is inestimable. Their helplessness has been compounded by the fact that most are petty traders or daily wagers, whose livelihoods were crushed both by the carnage and the lockdown that came close on its heels.[198] They were bereft of both the financial and social capital to make themselves heard.

The targeting of Muslim residents of North East Delhi was followed by the filing of criminal cases against young Muslim activists, including Jamia University student leaders Meeran Haider and Safoora Zargar—who was pregnant—and the charismatic youth leader Umar Khalid. They were all charged under the draconian Unlawful Activities Prevention Act (UAPA).

To the Muslims of riot-stricken North East Delhi, the pandemic brought multiple griefs: through the official Islamophobic narrative, the central government's anti-poor policies, the difficulties in rebuilding their broken lives after the communal violence, and topping all this, the indiscriminate arrests made by a highly communalized police force under cover of its 'riot investigation'. Every day, people helplessly bore witness to members of their community either being taken into custody or being assaulted by the police for breaking some lockdown rule or the other. 'I went out to buy vegetables for my home. I saw a fellow Muslim neighbour getting beaten up by the cops…I ran back to my house in fear and didn't get out for days,' said a resident of Mustafabad to my colleagues Varna and Meera. Another, an out-of-work labourer whose son had been arrested said despairingly, '*Kya karein? Inki Sarkar hai. Inki marzi hai. Humaare paas sirf duaaein hain.*' (What can we do? It is their government. Their will. We have only our prayers.)

In the claustrophobia of the lockdown, the anti-CAA movement, the magnificent peaceful democratic assertion that India witnessed through the winter of late 2019 and early 2020, was becoming a distant memory. Citizens across identities of religion, class, caste, gender and language had risen together to defend the secular spirit of India's Constitution. The popular movement, unprecedented in scale and moral salience since the freedom struggle, had badly rattled the ruling establishment by striking at the heart of its majoritarian project. It is evident that the establishment used the near-emergency lockdown situation to fight back hard. It cynically used the crisis of the pandemic to try to kill all dissent, and to create an alternative mythology, that Muslims are the enemy—not only determined to 'break India', but also responsible for super-spreading a deadly virus with the intent of destroying the nation and killing every non-Muslim. What greater proof could there be, then, that Muslims were fundamentally anti-India? No greater justification would be needed for laws designed to expel them from the country or lock them up in detention centres.

10

The Lockdown and Public Health: Myth and Reality

There was only one rationale possible for the closure of the entire economy, at immense human cost, through an authoritarian nationwide lockdown—that it would give India the window to greatly expand its health infrastructure in order to deal with the anticipated surge in the number of patients requiring testing, quarantine, treatment and care.

The government itself has not been transparent about how much it actually scaled up the available infrastructure. But there is ample evidence that it did *not* use the time of the lockdown to fill the enormous gaps in public health capacities, such as hospital beds, facilities for intensive care, ventilators, oxygen cylinders, PPEs and spaces for safe quarantine.

When the Prime Minister announced (on April 14) that 'we have created one lakh beds',[199] he was being less than truthful. The fact is that the government had mostly just repurposed the existing health system beds. In anticipation of an epidemic, you don't simply empty out public hospitals and make beds available for COVID cases by pushing out existing patients suffering from other illnesses. There was a shocking report, for instance, of cancer patients from two Mumbai hospitals being shifted out; they were forced to sleep on floor mats under a bridge.[200] Not only this, people coming to hospitals with ailments other than the Coronavirus infection were now denied beds. Apart from such unconscionable diversions which would cost many lives, there was no serious effort to prepare for the medical emergency. Two out of three districts in the country lacked any testing facilities even two months after the lockdown. Seven months into the pandemic, many parts of the country were reporting a shortage of medical oxygen.

In the early months, in Delhi, as in cities and towns across the country, people in need of emergency care for the Coronavirus infection and other medical conditions searched hopelessly for beds. Many were turned away by hospital after hospital, and many others waited for hours to be admitted and attended to. Several of them died. Delhi government officials announced in early June that by the end of July Delhi would need 80,000 additional hospital beds in view of the rapidly rising Coronavirus cases in the city. Soon after, Union Home Minister Amit Shah made a dramatic, highly publicized intervention, and plans were announced to create COVID-care spaces in stadiums, train compartments, banquet halls and hotels. The media that broadcast this news widely did not ask why these additional facilities had not been created during the punishing lockdown; and if these could be created after the country was unlocked, then why did we need to suffer the lockdown in the first place. Even now, the intention seemed to be only to manage the headlines. Beyond grand announcements, few people appeared to be serious about dealing with the crisis. When the first makeshift quarantine centre opened in a railway coach at Ashok Vihar Station, officials found that it was too hot for patients.[201] Temperatures soar to over 40 degrees Celsius in Delhi in July; railway coaches are made of metal and they stand not in sheds or the shade of giant trees but under the open sky. One would expect that ensuring they would be comfortable for patients expected to isolate themselves inside these coaches would have been among the first priorities. But perhaps this should not surprise us—after all, the patients in these makeshift isolation wards were unlikely to be from the affluent classes.

The situation was not much different in Maharashtra, Tamil Nadu, Gujarat, Karnataka and Uttar Pradesh, where, too, a massive demand for beds was expected by July. But even if new hospitals and ICU beds were indeed created, there were not enough health personnel. As officials in Mumbai said, 'Having more beds now is like putting band-aid on a fractured hand. We don't have enough health personnel, doctors, nurses, for the new patients coming in.'[202]

The tragedies of the poor must assume epic proportions before they will be noticed, even if nothing is done to alleviate their suffering—as the forced mass exodus of migrant workers proved. But even middle-class patients began to lose their lives as hospital after hospital refused them admission, and then the condition of government hospitals, where the economically disadvantaged come for treatment, also began to be noticed by the mainstream media. There were reports and images of patients made to lie between unattended corpses; families being given the wrong body to cremate; infected patients shunned by medical staff dying in unattended hospital toilets. Doctors and nurses complained about no safety equipment and not being paid their salaries for months. Bills were criminally inflated by private hospitals unregulated by the state, and corruption was evident in the purchase of essential equipment.

Within weeks of the loosening of the lockdown, more reports began to pour in of hundreds of patients unable to find beds in hospitals even in big cities where most professional medical services are concentrated. In Delhi, a family with a seriously ill COVID-19 patient was refused admission by four private hospitals (one of them asked for 10 lakh rupees) and then by a government hospital, outside which he finally died.[203] In Delhi, again, a young man made the rounds of several doctors and hospitals, made over 50 calls and sent desperate emails seeking help when his father developed very high fever. Defeated, he finally decided to try his luck outside the capital and somehow booked a seat for his father on a train to Bhopal. No one checked the visibly unwell man's fever on the way. Bhopal was better, and he got both an ICU bed and a ventilator but it turned out to be too late.[204] A factory worker in Noida took his 30-year-old pregnant wife in an auto-rickshaw in the summer heat to eight hospitals over 15 hours but each refused her admission because she had COVID-like symptoms, and she eventually died.[205] Another 24-year-old pregnant woman died after she was refused admission by four hospitals in Dehradun, because doctors feared her fever might mean COVID.[206] An elderly man died after six government hospitals in Delhi refused to admit him, saying they had no beds, even though a government app showed beds were available. A private hospital was not an option because the family could not afford the fee.[207] Families of patients in some COVID-designated hospitals in the capital spoke of nightmarish neglect of the patients by the health personnel who refused to touch them. Often no hospital staff were available to give the patients water or their meals on time, or to help those who were breathless to walk up to the washroom. Families had no option but to risk infection by entering the isolation wards to take care of their loved ones. Baljeet Shah, a resident of East Delhi who had been attending to his mother for a week in a government hospital told Vijayta Lalwani of *Scroll* that his mother needed oxygen at night but the nurses on duty would not enter the ward because they had no PPE kit. Even when a nurse did help with the oxygen, patients still needed someone from their families to assist them. 'They [hospital staff] leave the food outside the ward. Those who can get up will go but how will those on oxygen go to take the food?' Baljeet said.[208]

In Mumbai, which, like Delhi, boasts high-end private hospitals with 'world-class' facilities, the pandemic laid bare the city's poor health infrastructure. As the COVID cases rose, hospitals ran out of beds. A 55-year-old resident of Jogeshwari, suffering breathlessness and chest pain, was refused admission by six hospitals and died on a wheelchair in the seventh while waiting for a bed. In public hospitals, Coronavirus patients were asked to share beds, sleep on the floor in the corridors, or share wards with corpses that had not been removed because families refused to claim them and the hospital authorities hadn't figured out how to deal with the situation. Getting to even these ill-equipped and mismanaged hospitals was not easy. An asymptomatic 69-year-old diabetic discovered he was COVID positive when he was tested before his gallbladder surgery. In home quarantine, his sons found his oxygen levels falling dangerously and rang the official helpline to find a hospital bed. A dozen hospitals refused before one private hospital agreed to admit him. The next challenge was to get him an ambulance. They tried the official ambulance helpline, no one answered. They tried private services for an ambulance, none was available. They finally decided to transport him in their car, but he died as they were carrying him to it. A woman in Khar tested positive for COVID at a private clinic where she was being treated for encephalitis. The official helpline took 24 hours to find her an ICU bed in a COVID hospital. It then took some hours to get an ambulance, by which time the ICU bed had been given to another patient. The woman was admitted in the general ward despite her serious condition and she died within a few hours. According to a report on *Scroll*, in June, when COVID cases were rising exponentially in Mumbai, the government's 108 helpline had only 100 ambulances. Private ambulance services were charging 10,000 to 12,000 rupees to move a patient.[209] It is beyond comprehension why the number of ambulances were not increased massively to deal with the COVID emergency.

The bedlam at times could seem farcical if it were not so tragic: Monkeys stole COVID blood samples in Meerut;[210] 35 persons who were tested positive by private laboratories in Noida and sent to quarantine centres turned out to be negative when they were retested by government laboratories;[211] a family in Delhi was handed the wrong body and buried it thinking it was their father;[212] a similar 'mix-up' happened at least twice in Ahmedabad and twice in Hyderabad.[213]

Even the Supreme Court, not known in recent times to

criticize the government, declared the conditions of hospitals in Delhi as 'deplorable' and 'pathetic'. It spoke of COVID patients running from pillar to post to get admitted to hospitals even as a large number of beds lay vacant. It also observed: 'Patients are in the wards and the dead bodies are also in the same wards. Dead bodies are seen also in the lobby and waiting area. The patients were not supplied with any oxygen support or any other support, [there were] no saline drips...with the beds and there was no one to attend the patients.' The Solicitor General, appearing for the government, admitted that corpses had been found lying with patients, and that there had been instances of bodies being dragged with rope. The court also referred to dead bodies 'found in the garbage'.[214]

After a harrowing search for hospital beds, being caught in a hospital fire, surviving a fortnight in an ill-managed ICU and being presented with a shockingly inflated bill, one patient laments, 'We have been abandoned by our government.'[215]

My father is 94, my grandson just under two. I must confess that I was terrified at the prospect of either of them, or any member of my family, showing symptoms of COVID-19. I was not confident that I would even be able to get them tested, and find a hospital bed, let alone a ventilator. I was worried for my friends and my colleagues.

But I was—and at the time of writing continue to be—even more worried for the much larger family I have adopted over many years, of street children, homeless women and men and survivors of hate crimes, many of whom are battling TB. If middle-class people with abundant social capital were struggling to get their families tested and treated, what chance in hell was there for the destitute and the working poor? The cost of these official failures would be the loss of thousands of lives, invisible deaths which we could have prevented by humane and competent governance.

In one of the rare incidents of violence as resistance in the entire lockdown in the entire country, an altercation broke out between those serving food and a few of the thousands of destitute men in Yamuna Pushta, the settlement of homeless men on the banks of the Yamuna river in North Delhi that I have described earlier. The homeless men charged the staff distributing food at a temporary shelter with disrespect. The dispute escalated because one man jumped into the river and drowned. This ultimately led to some of the men setting the shelter on fire in their humiliation and rage. In retaliation, the administration forcibly vacated the entire settlement and herded the homeless men into school buildings which, schools being shut, had been converted into crowded quarantine centres. Before the homeless men were forced into these centres, their temperature was checked. I met one of them some weeks later, a casual worker from Jalpaiguri in Bengal who was unfortunate enough to have a fever that day. This man—whom I will call S, to protect his identity—spoke to me of the nightmare of the next four days.

The men who had fever were shifted to a government hospital, where their samples were taken. But they were told that they would have to remain in the hospital until their results came, four days later. Two men were made to share a single bed. This was the case for all patients, even those who were already in the hospital when S and the others were brought there. Some beds had patients who had died but no one wanted to handle their bodies. The nursing staff and ward boys were unwilling to touch any of the patients, either, and forced hapless impoverished men like S to handle other patients without any protective gear. Four days later, S tested negative. That night, he ran away from the hospital. He trudged many miles to the banks of the Yamuna, dodging the police. There he would encounter about twenty other homeless men who had also escaped like him. They would sleep in some Hume pipes at night, and hide from the police in the day, moving around by stealth to find some scraps of food, but often failing to. Yet they preferred this state to being in hospital or in a quarantine centre, about which they had heard terrible stories.

Where have we arrived as a nation?

*

India had a window of over a month and a half between its first reported infection and the nationwide lockdown. The first case of Coronavirus was detected in Kerala on 30 January 2020. This was a student who had returned from Wuhan, where the pandemic began. Even as late as 18 March, there were only 161 confirmed cases in the country, of which over 80% were in just six states: Maharashtra, Kerala, Haryana, Delhi, Uttar Pradesh and Karnataka.

There is little evidence that the Indian government used these precious weeks of low infection to strengthen its capacities for testing, tracing and cure; or to educate its people about precautions they could take, or prepare them for restrictions on movement and large gatherings that would become necessary. In fact, there were no advisories at all about avoiding large gatherings. Instead, the union government was occupied with sectarian politics in Delhi and Madhya Pradesh, and the much-hyped state visit of US President Donald Trump. (In fact, Trump's visit brought large numbers of international visitors to India—at a time when only travellers from China and Hong Kong were being screened at a few Indian airports—and over one lakh people gathered to listen to Trump's speech inside a single stadium.)

For a report that appeared on the site *Article 14*, Nitin Sethi and Kumar Sambhav Shrivastava of the Reporters Collective accessed official documents which show that despite clear warnings of the dangers from the advancing pandemic from its own scientists in February, the Indian government did not put in place a testing and surveillance strategy against the COVID-19 outbreak until the end of March.[216] There is mounting, and highly damning, evidence that scientific advice was consistently ignored or not sought when decisions were taken to impose the largest lockdown in history with no notice, or when the lockdown was extended twice. There were many warnings given, for instance, by health experts who were part of the COVID-19 task force. Advising strongly against a China-like lockdown in India, one of the papers written by these experts said: 'Instead of coercive top-down quarantine approaches, which are driven by the authorities, community and civil-society led self-quarantine and self-monitoring could emerge as more sustainable and implementable strategies in a protracted pandemic like COVID-19.'[217] One of the scientists who authored the studies cited above told *Article 14*, on condition of anonymity, that a nationwide lockdown was not the same as quarantine or social isolation. 'In Indian conditions such a lockdown provides social isolation for only the rich who live in less dense and high-floor space areas,' he said. 'To some degree it can protect them from the spread. But, for the poor, without high levels of door-to-door screening and the fastest possible quarantining of those found positive, a lockdown will only help the virus spread intra-community.'

The scientist went on to explain that the urban poor, who almost always live in densely populated areas, 'share very small physical spaces, [they] live with common facilities, such as public toilets. The lockdown has forced likely COVID-19 patients to share these spaces for weeks with others. Imagine if one COVID positive person is sharing a community toilet with hundreds, if not thousands, daily, spreading the virus, and the coercive lockdown is only restraining him (sic) from going to the authorities…'

But it is apparent that none of these warnings and advice was given credence by the government, at immense cost to impoverished populations and the economy. These warnings were issued before these experts were put on the COVID Task Force. But even after they were constituted into a task force comprising 21 leading scientists from around the country, with an extensive mandate to guide official decision-making about dealing with the pandemic, they were not consulted before critical decisions such as the extension of the lockdown were taken. On condition of anonymity again (which also says something about the nature of the authorities the task force answers to), one member said to *Caravan* magazine that it seemed to him that the committee was constituted only to give the impression that scientists were being consulted, but not to actually seek or act on the basis of their advice. He gave the example of permitting private laboratories to test for COVID-19 and to fix an unreasonably high price ceiling of Rs 4,500 per test when it should not cost more than Rs 500.

The Supreme Court, in one of its few progressive rulings, directed that all laboratories should be required to provide free COVID testing, but the government intervened and persuaded it to permit private testing for a fee.[218]

The third lockdown was also imposed without seeking the advice of the expert committee, and members again said privately to *Caravan* that even those who supported the idea of the initial lockdown would have opposed its extension as it served no further purpose.[219]

Having ignored its own scientists, the union government did not seek the opinion and advice of chief ministers or health ministers of states, either. Chief ministers were contacted by the prime minister through video conferencing only *after* he had announced the lockdown. It is still a secret who exactly the prime minister consulted before he decided to plunge the country into the largest and most stringent lockdown that the world has ever seen.

Legal philosopher Upendra Baxi underlines the importance of humility, or the willingness of state actors to consult, learn and make rapid course-correction, because of the uncertainty of knowledge about how to deal with the pandemic. This requires us all to learn from and listen to each other, and not take recourse to antagonistic politics that divides people into 'friend' and 'enemy'. It entails what Baxi calls 'resilient politics based on empathy'.[220] However, the Indian government displayed not humility but immense hubris.

*

Global experience has shown that planned lockdowns may indeed have helped some countries to better deal with the pandemic crisis by giving them time to mobilise resources, set up systems for case tracking and make preparations to handle the rush of cases needing institutional care. The evidence for India, as we have seen, is that even a lockdown for which the Indian people have paid immeasurably was substantially squandered. The government lacked the vision, the capability and the compassion to steer its people through the tempest.

The review of official records by Nitin Sethi and Kumar Sambhav published in *Article 14* (cited above) has also clearly established that even after the lockdown had been imposed, scientists working for the union government were warning that the lockdown would have limited impact on the spread of the virus, 'preventing only 20-25% of infections that might eventually be detected at the peak of the pandemic'. Even this effect, they said, would be 'temporary', unless urgent, scientifically rigorous measures were taken to curtail the pandemic. They recommended ramping up testing and quarantining facilities, putting in place nationwide monitoring mechanisms, rapidly increasing the number of intensive-care units and hospital beds and arranging enough protective resources for health-care workers. They also recommended 'door-to-door supply of food and essential items to the poor'. As we have seen, the government did not act on any of these recommendations: On 24 April, a month after the lockdown, India's testing rate was among the lowest in the world—380 persons per million of the population, when the global average for that day was 5,897 per million.[221] As late as 4 August, WHO's chief scientist, Soumya Swaminathan, was expressing the organisation's unhappiness with India's testing rate, saying it was one of the lowest in the world—

just 2.08 crore of the total population of 138 crores had been tested, which is about 1.5%. Without adequate testing, Swaminathan said, combating the Coronavirus is like 'fighting fire blindfolded'.[222]

Sethi and Shrivastava write that 'having imposed an unplanned lockdown, the government was not prepared even with testing protocols to track down those infected with the Coronavirus...Confusion apparently prevailed, and experts expressed their frustration at the lack of action, despite prior advice'.[223] There was, and continued to be, shocking and tragic shortage of hospital beds, ventilators and ICU facilities even in mega cities like Mumbai and Delhi, as we have already noted.

'There is no doubt in my mind that the lockdown has failed,' an epidemiologist who is also a member of the task force told *Caravan*. 'Lockdown as a tool only makes sense if you have the backup of laboratories, and shore up testing. Without testing, it is like having a revolver, but with no bullet in it. Any sensible policymaker would have looked at the data, taken some time to think about it, plan effectively what we should do, why, and how—before implementing the first lockdown.' Another expert said, 'The rationale for lockdown was to buy time to prepare ourselves in terms of logistics, preparing our hospitals, preparing our manpower, preparing guidelines, standard operating procedures.' But little of this was done. Several public-health experts whom *Caravan* spoke to said the government failed to use the time to expand contact tracing, massively scale up testing, and ramp up India's medical infrastructure for the pandemic.[224] The government did not even do something as basic as forecasting the demand for PPE kits, as had been recommended by the WHO.[225]

The task force epidemiologist was unequivocal that a lockdown does not stop transmission in any way, it just slows it down. 'It does not add any extra value other than ensuring forcible social distancing,' he told *Caravan*. 'That has shown results in the first world, where population density is far less than in a country like ours. It is of no use to place blame (on) people, especially in cities where so many are homeless—where were you going to lockdown the homeless families? Around 20 per cent of (the) population in any big city lives in slums.'[226] The numbers are actually much higher than 20 per cent, as we observed in an earlier chapter.

Another member of the task force went further and said the central government's response to the pandemic had actually made the situation worse. He listed the government's failures: '[Failure in] containing spread to multiple sites in the country…On (the) political and administrative front, in providing social services to people under lockdown and [to] migrants…[F]ailure of risk communication and countering stigma.' UN advisor Sunil Panakandan said countries like South Korea used limited lockdowns as a public health measure and succeeded; India used it as a law and order measure and failed. Marc Lipsitch, a Harvard epidemiologist deploys a powerful metaphor, that lockdown as a pandemic response is like getting to a 'life raft' without solving the bigger problem: how to get to the shore?[227]

It defies understanding why the union government chose not to rely and build upon the considerable talent and experience of handling epidemics that is available both within and outside government. Instead of asking epidemiologists and public-health specialists to lead the country on its public-health strategies on the pandemic, it appointed a clinical paediatrician, Dr V.K. Paul—a member of the NITI Aayog, created and headed by Prime Minister Narendra Modi—as chairperson of the 21-member COVID-19 task force and also as chairperson of the first empowered group to oversee 'the medical emergency management plan'. Sujatha Rao, former union Health Secretary, in a discussion organized by the Centre for Equity Studies on the pandemic,[228] affirmed that India has a rich experience of successful public health strategies to overcome HIV and polio; but this learning was set aside, epidemiologists were marginalized, and crucial decision-making was placed in the hands of clinicians.

T. Sunderaraman, a leading public-health practitioner and teacher, made a similar point, about ignoring and side-lining the significant knowledge and capacity which the Indian state has built up over the years to deal with epidemics. There has been a consistent watering down of the already existing public health systems, he said. We have a system which was built after swine flu in 2010, and this is the Integrated Disease Surveillance Programme (IDSP). In early February 2020, the IDSP presented its report in which it faithfully and brilliantly reported the first three COVID-19 cases in India. And then, without any explanation, the IDSP was side-lined and no further reports were issued by it. Decisions were taken instead by officials who are not familiar with epidemiology or public health.

In a press briefing on 24 April, Dr V.K. Paul presented a slide with a graph that ambitiously claimed that India would see no new cases of COVID-19 after 16 May. As Vidya Krishnan wrote in *Caravan* magazine, 'In the graph the number of new cases dived in drastic fashion, in perfect alignment with the Modi administration's lockdown dates.'[229]

Paul declared, 'The country has shown that the lockdown was effective.' Soon after the briefing, the Press Information Bureau (PIB), of the Government of India, tweeted the graph and quoted Paul: 'No need to fear hidden spike in #COVID cases, the disease is in control.' Experts and dispassionate observers across the country and the world were aghast. An epidemiologist, also a member of the national task force, told Krishnan the slide Paul presented was 'wildly inaccurate'. 'We have been meeting daily but we were never consulted on this study,' he said.

By 16 May, the number of cases in India had in fact surged to 85,940. Three days later, the figure crossed the one lakh mark. On 22 May, when the number of recorded positive cases had risen to 1,18,447 and 3,583 deaths had been reported, Paul finally apologised for the 'misconception' caused by the graph.

This reflects three problems. The first, as we have mentioned, is that despite enormous talent available both inside and outside government, it chooses to side-line it. The second—perhaps the biggest problem—which is directly related to this, is the PMO-centric, or rather PM-centric, nature of the COVID-19, and indeed every other, task force. Quoting a senior bureaucrat in a laudatory story on 'PM Modi's task force', the deputy editor of a national magazine wrote: 'This task force, with handpicked bureaucrats and key officials, operates around the powerful Prime Minister's Office…the PM has the final say in each and every decision after the information is collated and placed before him for advice. "Most instructions come from the PM," says a secretary-level officer. "Even in technical matters, his vision and knowledge are exemplary. We always feel he is ahead of us.'"[230] What hope can there be for professional, scientific crisis management, which requires discussion and frequent course-correction, in an atmosphere of such authoritarianism and such sycophancy?

The third problem is an old one with the Modi government—that it routinely suppresses data of any kind which does not show government efforts in a rosy light, and in its place makes grand generalized claims with no empirical basis (such as that we will double farm income in five years and create two crore new jobs a year). Contrast this with transparency which helped countries like South Korea, Germany and New Zealand to successfully combat the contagion. India incentivized hiding bad news because those who showed higher numbers of infections were seen as under-performing, while actually they may have been identifying more cases by higher testing and tracing.

*

Experts tell us that across the world, clear, unambiguous messaging is indeed one of the factors that has helped achieve some flattening of the curve—that is, slowing down the number of daily new cases.

In India, as we have seen, official communication has been abysmal, and among the primary reasons for this is PM Narendra Modi's contempt for democratic, open and responsive communication, his deep distrust of anyone who does not bow low to his wisdom, and his hostility towards anyone who might ask him questions or offer suggestions as an equal. As we have noted, he is perhaps the only head of government in the world who has not held a single press conference during the pandemic. In contrast, the leaders of

New Zealand, Germany, Taiwan and other countries which have done exceptionally well in containing the spread of the pandemic engaged sensitively and honestly with their fellow citizens through almost daily briefings—to which they came prepared with clear, reliable information; and prepared to listen and answer questions.

The Indian Prime Minister made three one-way-communication national broadcasts during the lockdown. He spoke long and sometimes ramblingly on each occasion, often using Hindu imagery, but he was economical in giving concrete details of what the government was doing and why. He never explained why the lockdown and its repeated extensions were necessary, nor what the government had achieved during this time in tangible terms. In the last of his speeches about the lockdown extension, when the distress of migrants and joblessness were peaking and the number of infections spiralling dangerously, he dwelled instead on the importance of economic self-reliance (Atmanirbhar Bharat), leading to a bitter response from some migrants that the government meant that they had to rely only on themselves during the pandemic and lockdown; the government would do nothing for them. And he mostly seemed to suggest that the suffering of the poor would have to be alleviated by the charity of those better off, their employers and landlords, and the general, munificent public. After this, as it became more and more apparent that India's COVID-19 strategy was proving to be a disaster, the PM just stopped communicating on the subject, leaving it to the chief ministers to do the heavy lifting.

You may rightly ask, what could he have done differently. I will try to answer that question toward the end of this book.

But some answers would already be apparent. He could have consulted widely and transparently—with epidemiologists, social scientists, public health experts, doctors with experience of working with the disadvantaged, chief ministers, collectives of workers, social workers and activists. He could also have looked at and learned from examples of successful and humane containment strategies among countries where the pandemic had spread before it reached India. He could have had open and several discussions with experts and workers' representatives to assess the impact of a total lockdown on the labouring poor, nine out of ten of whom are in the informal sector. This would have restrained him from imposing a nationwide lockdown. Instead, there could have been limited containment in big cities, but with the Public Distribution System (PDS) made universal and with the guarantee of full payment of statutory minimum wage (around 7000 rupees a month per household) to everyone whose livelihood would be interrupted by even the limited, localised containment. He could have nationalized private healthcare for the duration of the pandemic, greatly ramped up testing facilities, and involved the states, municipalities, panchayats and other local collectives in a rigorous policy of testing, contact tracing and isolation, while ensuring that public quarantine and isolation facilities for the rich and the poor were exactly the same. He could have taken steps to add many more hospital beds by redeploying infrastructure like stadiums and universities, but ensuring that healthcare for other ailments was not compromised in any way. He could have emptied out the country's overcrowded jails, shored up support for mental health and domestic violence distress…

I could go on.

The prime minister could also, crucially, have communicated regularly and frequently through press-conferences, taking questions, and explaining his government's decisions with empathy, transparency and respect. Instead, the daily briefings of the Government of India were mainly by a joint secretary-level civil servant. The communications by this officer have been criticised for being opaque, lacking vital information, and some ducking and stonewalling.[231] In the name of social distancing most journalists were barred from attending these briefings. Eventually, only reporters from the state-run television channel Doordarshan and the news agency Asian News International were invited. To crucial questions about the logistics of preparation for the pandemic, the joint secretary would respond with vague statements like '*Kaam ho raha hai*' (Work is going on). To a question in late March—immediately after the lockdown was imposed—about whether India was experiencing 'community transmission', he replied that we should ban that term. When journalists would ask questions such as where were the 'hotspots', how many patients were on ventilator, etc., the response from the official would always be vague and confounding. These press briefings also facilitated the unconscionable communalisation of the pandemic by separately announcing the number of cases which had originated from the Tablighi Jamaat gathering in Delhi and using this to whip up hatred against Muslims as malign super-spreaders of the infection. From 24 April, the Indian Council of Medical Research (ICMR) representative who was hitherto part of the daily briefings stopped attending. What this meant was that the one expert with domain expertise relevant to the crisis was no longer available to answer questions of a technical nature. Eventually, on 11 May, the daily briefings were stopped altogether. The media was told that the government had decided to limit the number of briefings and have them 'as and when required'.[232]

Official communications were also often contradictory and confusing, with different messages coming from the centre and from states with non-BJP governments—messages that were all thin on vital details such as the methods of testing and containment and the line of treatment, directives on manufacturing and procuring of PPEs, the actual numbers of new hospital beds, testing kits and ventilators, etc. [233] The chaos created by conflicting and rapidly changing orders and guidelines was particularly acute in Delhi, as there was a clear lack of coordination and agreement between the union and Delhi state governments (until Union Home Minister Amit Shah chose to intervene and the otherwise mercurial Arvind Kejriwal, chief minister of Delhi, suddenly and inexplicably fell completely in line).

The ICMR website shows that in a span of five months—from March to July—the medical research body (presided over by the Union Health Minister) modified testing criteria six times. Health workers and persons desiring to be tested found it difficult to keep pace with the changing guidelines.[234] It was only from 9 April, when the number of infections detected had reached almost 6000, that the research body allowed testing of all individuals showing symptoms of Severe Acute Respiratory Infection. Before this testing was restricted to those with symptoms and international travel history, health workers and contacts of confirmed cases. On 2 June, the Delhi government altered these ICMR guidelines 'to rule out testing asymptomatic people, except if they had comorbidities or were over the age of 60.'[235] The Delhi government also issued show cause notices to eight private labs which were testing asymptomatic cases, and barred them from further testing. This brought down the overall testing capacity in Delhi at a time when cases were rising.[236] On 8 June, the central-government-appointed Lieutenant Governor of Delhi set aside the Delhi government order and asked it to follow ICMR guidelines. Two petitions were filed in the Delhi High Court complaining that 'multiple orders from Delhi government and then the LG [were] leading to confusion among the doctors as well as the general public.'[237] The Delhi High Court then ordered the Delhi government to follow ICMR guidelines and reprimanded it for low number of tests.

The confused and confusing changes and the earlier restrictions to testing in these guidelines were not explained on any scientific grounds. As a result, symptomatic patients and their contacts were constantly turned away and India was testing well below its capacity to test (which was already very low compared to countries which were effectively controlling the spread of). It is difficult not to conclude that the priority of governments, both at the centre and in Delhi and other states, was to deal with the optics and to manage perceptions rather than fight the infection head-on.

Similar confusion prevailed regarding quarantine rules. In middle of June the LG of Delhi ordered that all positive cases would have to mandatorily spend five days in government quarantine facilities, reversing the earlier policy of home quarantine. This evoked sharp criticism from the Delhi government, which said that this order would discourage people from getting tested. Eventually the LG withdrew his order, only to come back with a fresh directive that all positive cases must visit a government COVID centre where there would be an assessment whether they should remain in home quarantine or be sent to a government-run centres. This spawned huge logistical problems regarding how the positive cases would travel to these government-run centres, and whether such movement would lead to further spreading the infection—government ambulances were limited and difficult to access, and private ambulances were charging astronomical rates. The Delhi government then wrote to the Union Home Minister, demanding the revocation of the LG's order, which was finally done because of the logistical nightmare it was leading to. The scientific usefulness of these competing and contradictory orders was never clarified.

There were similar contradictions in rules related to inter-state movement and quarantine, at a time when millions of migrants were walking back to their homes. An editorial in *The Hindu* observed: 'The Centre, as the lockdown regulator, now has the important task of creating a consensus with the states on the quarantine modalities. Confusion surrounding quarantine for passengers who took the first relief trains from New Delhi to various cities, leading to some of them returning to the national capital, underscores the need for agreement. The response so far has been flat-footed in several states. Train passengers arriving in Bengaluru protested that they received no advance notice of institutional quarantine, although they were given an option to stay in hotels for 14 days incurring considerable expenditure. Labourers compulsorily quarantined in Uttar Pradesh and Bihar escaped from the facilities after complaining of bad conditions. In Kerala, the Centre insists on a 14-day institutional quarantine for those arriving by air, rejecting the state's proposal for seven days in a public facility and another seven at home; train passengers were given a home quarantine option. Such a lack of certitude…reflects failure at building consensus.'[238]

Similar conflict and confusion prevailed between neighbouring states on opening of borders, which led to enormous hardships for migrant workers returning home. So at one time when Haryana opened its borders allowing movement based on MHA guidelines, Delhi sealed them citing a surge in cases.[239] In another instance, following tragic deaths of migrant workers in road and train accidents, Uttar Pradesh suddenly barred movement on foot and also in trucks, lorries etc., advising the workers to travel in trains and buses instead.[240] This order was unmindful of the fact that lakhs of workers were already on the road and were now stranded at the border or on highways with no money and little food. While some of them were rounded up and locked up by the UP government in sub-human makeshift shelters, others escaped the fate by escaping through canals and deserted fields.

To make matters worse, from the very beginning of the pandemic, there was a flood of fake messages and unscientific miscommunications—which some people have called an 'infodemic'.[241] Government officials and scientists were intimidated by the lobbies of 'traditional' medicine who used their proximity to political power to promote their business interests and often regressive agendas by claiming that physical yoga, ayurvedic diets and therapies like applying cow-dung on the body or drinking cow urine could cure a Coronavirus infection. The government and its scientists did little to clarify that none of these claims were supported by modern medical science, none had ever even been tested. Without any scientific data to back it up, the government's AYUSH ministry recommended homeopathic and ayurvedic cures for COVID-19.[242] Similarly, the Gujarat government distributed homeopathy pills and Ayurvedic mixtures in hotspots.[243]

Former union health secretary Sujatha Rao and many others have also questioned how decisions were made during the lockdown about what to allow and what to prohibit. Rarely was any scientific explanation offered, say, about why private cars were allowed but not taxis. A classic example was the dusk to dawn curfew even after the country began unlocking during the day. Was it that the government had access to some unknown scientific studies that proved the virus was more deadly in the dark? Or was it just that it confused a riot curfew (in which ensuring everyone stays indoors at night makes eminent sense) with a health emergency?

*

Such confusion and tardiness, together with a disdain for science and obsession with headline management, was also behind India's extremely low levels of testing. This has been, arguably, India's greatest failure in battling the pandemic. Instead of attempting containment of COVID-19 through the blunt and brutal weapon of the lockdown, the experience of South Korea should have convinced us that the smartest and least hazardous strategy is extensive testing and contact tracing. Given our vast network of primary health care workers, this should have been possible. Timely testing is crucial as it allows an infected person—who may or may not be symptomatic—to be isolated to avoid infecting others and quickly receive the care s/he needs. It is also crucial for people and governments to understand the actual prevalence of the disease, rather than under-reporting the bad news.

India's testing rate, as we have seen, was abysmally low at the start of the lockdown, and remained low during the lockdown and even after it was lifted. After two months of the lockdown it was at 2000 tests per million, against over 65,000 for Spain, 38,000 for Germany and the US, and 21,000 for France. Moreover, as experts pointed out, the India figure was misleading because it included multiple tests for the same person, which meant that the number of persons being tested per million was even less than 2000. As the number of infections surged and India became the country with the third highest number of Corona positive cases in the world, the government finally admitted that testing would have to be ramped up urgently. In late July the government announced a daily target of 10 lakh, or one million, tests per day for the next two months. As we have seen, by mid-August India was still way behind countries with a comparable caseload, like the USA and Brazil.

For months, India chose to deal with its low capacity to test not by massively sourcing and producing testing kits, but by, in effect, reducing greatly the demand for the kits by pegging its testing criteria very narrowly. As we have seen, only those with international travel history and health professionals working in COVID wards were being tested initially. This approach led to the numbers of officially reported cases being low, creating a false sense of security. It displayed the government's efforts in a favourable light by perilously hiding the true extent of the spread of the infection.

The question of which tests should be conducted and how also remained highly confused and opaque, even potentially dangerous. At first the ICMR heavily leaned on antibody tests, which reveal if a person has been infected in the recent past. Antibody testing kits were being sourced from a Chinese company for this, until details emerged that pointed to possible corruption. It was only because of what *Caravan* reporter Vidya Krishnan describes as 'inadvertent whistle-blowing'—resulting from a dispute between three private companies over the distribution of the antibody kits—that it came to light that the union government had 'allowed the costs of the COVID-19 antibody tests to be inflated by nearly 145 per cent'. This was struck down by the Delhi High Court, which disclosed the details in its judgement: ICMR had offered to pay Rs 30 crorc for five lakh test kitsse at an inflated price that would have given the intermediary companies a profit of Rs 18.75 crore. Following the judgement, the government cancelled the procurement order for the test kits. But to compound matters, the kits turned out also to be unreliable. The day after the court's ruling, ICMR issued an advisory to all state governments not to purchase kits from the Chinese company because these had given inaccurate results. There was no explanation as to why the union government had placed such a large order, at massively inflated costs, for unreliable test kits in the first place.[244] It is a commentary on the mainstream media, the political opposition and the judiciary that no one has been held criminally accountable for such corruption at a time of the worst pandemic in a century that threatens the lives of tens of thousands of people in the country.

While a red-faced ICMR quickly recalled the faulty kits, it also shifted to rapid diagnostic or rapid antigen tests, scrapping antibody tests. States were left confused, and uncertain about how to procure the new kits. Besides, the antibody tests had been crucial to their containment strategies. As the health minister of Chhattisgarh told *Caravan*, 'The antibody kit is an advanced surveillance tool, and we need it to make informed decisions. If we need to know which areas in the state are badly affected, we need these kits.' Experts have always had concerns about the rapid antigen tests. They give faster results but are also less reliable, with an accuracy rate that can be as low as 30 per cent. According to Professor K Srinath Reddy of the Public Health Foundation of India, 'The antigen test will miss more than half of truly infected cases.'[245]

Finally, ICMR issued guidelines requiring those with negative results from an antigen test to *also* get the more accurate RT-PCR test done if they showed any symptoms. Meanwhile, private companies were allowed to charge up to Rs 4,500 for the RT-PCR test.

More dangerously, even as the infection began to spread into small towns and rural India, large parts of the country had no testing facilities. Even two months after the lockdown, over two-thirds of the 630 districts that had at least one detected case had no COVID testing laboratories within their boundaries. Only a third of the country's districts (250 of a total of 736) had any testing facilities.[246] By the end of August, the number of government testing laboratories across the country were still a low 998. By then, the infection was mounting in the small towns and villages of poorer states like Bihar, Jharkhand, Uttar Pradesh and Odisha. But these states had just 44, 33, 121 and 41 COVID testing laboratories, respectively.[247]

*

Speaking at the discussion on the pandemic organised by the Centre for Equity Studies that I have referred to before, Vikas Bajpai, who teaches public health at JNU, was most trenchant in his criticism of the lockdown. None of the consequences that followed were unforeseen, and yet the lockdown was enforced, wreaking terrible havoc on countlesslives. It reflects, he observed, a profound class bias, which explains the government strategy that had excluded, even in its very conception, the poor and the vulnerable. Among the harshest consequences of this class bias was the branding of the worst victims of this pandemic and lockdown as the primary and irresponsible transmitters of the virus. People who could not afford to comply with the cruel lockdown and came out in search of food or even the smallest chance of earning a wage were chased and beaten by the police. Migrants desperate to reach their villages were stopped and put into overcrowded, abominable quarantine facilities.

Journalist Radhika Bordia wrote a sensitive report for *The Wire* on quarantine centres set up in schools and homeless shelters in Delhi, where migrants stopped and picked up while trying to escape the city, and homeless people who had nowhere to run to, were kept by force.[248] She spoke to Pushpendra, a taxi driver who lost his work after the lockdown, and was caught by the police while trying to walk to his home in Bulandshahr. He was locked with about a hundred others, some with families and small children, in the Sarai Kale Khan homeless shelter. He had already spent 45 days in what he described as a jail. 'None of us were allowed to leave, sometimes not even allowed out for fresh air, but no one was able to tell us under what law they were holding us captive.' ['*Qaid kiya*' was the term he used.]

Nand Ram Ahirwal and his wife Leela from Lalitpur in Uttar Pradesh were working on a construction site in Delhi when the lockdown was imposed. Left without food and work, they tried to walk to Lalitpur with their four-year-old daughter, but they too were caught by the police. For almost a month and half now, Nand Ram had been begging the policemen at the quarantine centre to let them go home. 'I have been living like a *qaidi* (criminal) for no fault of mine,' he told Bordia. Leela said, 'Please take a look at the place where we go to get drinking water and then see the condition of the bathroom next to it.' She was interrupted and rebuked by a policeman who then turned to Bordia and said, 'These people are never satisfied with what they're given, it's in their nature, so don't take them seriously.' When he moved away, Leela said, in tears, 'We've lost jobs, we've run out of all our money, but the hardest thing is to be stripped of our dignity, to be made to feel like beggars...treated like prisoners.'

The conditions at most such centres across the country were appalling. They were overcrowded, the toilets were clogged, the food tasteless, and soap and sanitary napkins were a luxury. At a school converted into a quarantine centre in south Delhi, men spoke to Bordia about the humiliation they were subjected to every day. One of them said, 'We ran out of bathing soap five days ago, we had just one bar between seven people. When we asked them for more, we were told we should be grateful we're being fed.' Another man spoke of people being assaulted by the police with lathis each time they tried to come out of the shelter for a breath of fresh air. 'This feels like an endless prison term,' he said. 'But I'm told I should be grateful as it's for our safety. I'd rather die of a virus than tolerate the abuses I get here.'

These quarantine centres were set up ostensibly to prevent the spread of the contagion. But ironically, they were like hothouses most favourable for the rapid breeding and circulation of the virus. Had the migrants instead been allowed to leave for their villages at the start of the lockdown, their return facilitated by the government, when infection rates in the country were just a little over 500, very few in the countryside would have been infected. Now, after traumatic weeks locked up in these packed, unsanitary and undignified quarantine centres, when infection rates had soared to lakhs, the chances of these unfortunate migrants and homeless people being infected themselves and spreading the virus around the country was exponentially higher. Meanwhile, middle-class people with larger homes were allowed to quarantine at home, or, if you could afford the bills, in hotels.

*

India has a total of 11,54,686 registered allopathic doctors.[249] Of this, the government sector—which the current testing and treatment of the novel Coronavirus is mostly limited to—has 1,16,756 doctors. That amounts to one government doctor for every 10,926 persons. The WHO recommends a ratio of one doctor for every 1000 patients.[250] As Poonam Muttreja of The Population Foundation of India put it in an interview with *IndiaSpend*, 'The COVID-19 outbreak has pushed India's healthcare sector into ICU. Infrastructural inadequacies, shortage of human resources, lack of adequate funding and huge interstate and interregional variations in the availability of health services have been the major impediments in India's COVID-19-containment strategy.'[251] According to official data available in The National Health Profile for 2019, there are, in all, 7,13,986 government hospital beds available in India. This amounts to less than one bed—0.55, to be exact—per 1000 people. What is worse, in 12 states—including Bihar, Jharkhand, UP, Gujarat, MP, Odisha and Assam—which account for 70% of the country's population, the figure is even lower, ranging from 0.11 to 0.50 beds per 1000.[252] This isn't surprising given that, as Muttreja points out, public spending on health has been stuck at around 1% of GDP since 2004, and even faced with a massive health crisis, the government made no serious effort to start correcting this: 'The amount included in the fiscal stimulus for health is grossly insufficient. The increase in allocation announced on May 12 [2020] amounts to 0.008% of the country's GDP…It is not clear how this will be sufficient for opening infectious diseases hospital blocks in all districts, and public health laboratories at block levels.'[253]

India's public health response to the COVID-19 emergency has been significantly foreclosed because of the systematic neglect of public health under the influence of neoliberal policies in recent decades which have been nothing short of war on India's poor and disadvantaged. When India became independent in 1947, the private health sector provided only 5-10% of total patient care. Today it accounts for 82% of outpatient visits, and employment of 80% of doctors and 70% of nurses and midwives.[254] India spends only around 1.15% of its GDP on health, yet ranks among the top 20 of the world's countries in its private spending on health, at 4.2% of its GDP. Employers covering medical expenses of their staff accounts for 9% of this total spending on private care; health insurance accounts for 5-10%; and 82% is from people's personal funds. India has chosen to spend a significant part of its very low public investments in health to make insurance payments towards private healthcare. Estimates of middle-class income in India range from 10 to 50 US dollars per capita per day, and it is estimated that around 150 million—15 crore—people are part of this middle class. A vast majority of the remainder, around 800 million—80 crore—are poor, and out-of-pocket spending on health emergencies has been identified in numerous studies as one of the major reasons for people sinking deeper into poverty.

The primary reliance on for-profit private healthcare is actively promoted by state policy. In her 2020 budget speech, India's finance minister proposed handing over even government-run district hospitals to private medical colleges and offered land at concessional rates to facilitate this. Sixty per cent of public funds disbursed under the publicly funded health insurance programme called PM-JAY (Ayushman Pradhan Mantri Jan Arogya Yojana) already go to the private sector. Many field studies indicate that insurance has not significantly reduced the out-of-pocket spending on health by the poor.[255] If the state had ramped up its spending on health at least three or four times, and invested this in strengthening public health systems, instead, beginning with primary healthcare, this would have provided far greater protection to the poor.

Although the neo-liberal Indian state has chosen to place all its bets on the private sector, when we are hit by the greatest health emergency since Independence, the contribution of the private sector has been one of shameful abdication. Private hospitals, which account for two-thirds of hospital beds in India, and almost 80% of available ventilators, have been handling less than 10% of COVID-19 cases.[256] This may be partly because the government asked hospitals to stop outpatient departments and elective or non-emergency surgeries, as a result of which private hospitals around India reported a sharp drop in footfall and a severe financial squeeze. However, the main reason for the drop in patient admissions has been conscious withdrawal by the private hospitals because grasping the nettle of COVID-19 testing and treatment goes against their business model. Even though the Union Ministry of Health and Family Welfare issued guidelines on 26 March directing all hospitals to create separate wards for the isolation and treatment of COVID-19 patients, few private hospitals opted to offer such treatment. With Coronavirus infections spreading in hospitals through unknown carriers, some private hospitals even went to the extent of denying admission to *all* patients, except in a life-or-death situation (and, in practice, sometimes not even then). The Bihar government accused private hospitals in the state of completely withdrawing from the fight against COVID-19.[257]

Private health-care has let the people down in numerous ways during the pandemic. Its refusal to participate as an equal partner with the public sector in testing and treating patients is shocking enough. Even more shocking are reports of patients being turned away because they were poor and it was obvious that they could not pay, or because they were Muslim. And then there have been many news reports and considerable anecdotal evidence of hospitals greatly inflating costs of beds and treatment, preying on the dread. Treatment costs for diseases and medical conditions other than COVID have also soared in private hospitals. A patient seeking dialysis in a private Bangalore hospital used to pay 2,500 rupees a session; in June, as the pandemic worsened, he was charged 39,000 rupees a session, plus 10,000 rupees for an ambulance.[258] Patients were charged 10,000 rupees extra per day for PPE equipment by some private hospitals in Delhi, 8,900 rupees in Mumbai and 5,000 rupees in Chandigarh[259]; but *IndiaSpend* has calculated that the cost of one PPE set is 362 rupees, and at the most health personnel would need to use four such sets a day, amounting to 1,448 rupees.[260]

Dr Sakthivel Selvaraj of the Public Health Foundation of India (PHFI) sums up: 'India has perhaps the largest private healthcare market in the world, both in terms of financing and provision of care. Its inefficiency and inequity in healthcare is often more apparent than anywhere else. The current scenario under COVID-19 is only a reflection of the system in which the private sector hesitates and is unwilling to participate, leaving the hapless patients and the government to bear the burden. In an acute situation where private sector participation is far more required, their dithering and hands-off approach is not only callous but calls for a rethink on the part of the government to rejig its strategy of utilising taxpayers' money to procure healthcare services from them. COVID-19 is a wake-up call to move towards nationalisation of healthcare services.'[261]

I agree entirely. To my mind, in such a situation the only effective and equitable public policy response would be nationalisation, at least for the duration of the pandemic, of private health services, in the way Spain has done, making their entire personnel and infrastructure available for state deployment. But given the pro-business predilections of the government, this is most unlikely to happen.

The government has done little to regulate private hospitals, thus effectively encouraging extortion and criminal refusal to offer services. People who should be holding private establishments to account have in fact patronised them. Union Home Minister Amit Shah, in charge of the country's pandemic disaster response, tested positive for COVID-19 in early August and chose to be hospitalised at Medanta, a luxurious private hospital in Gurugram. (After his discharge, he was re-hospitalized, reportedly for pancreatitis, and this time he was admitted into the country's premier government facility, the All India Institute of Medical Sciences.) In June, the health minister of Delhi, Satyendra Jain, had also got himself admitted to an expensive private hospital when he tested positive, instead of a public hospital (where he no doubt would have been assured 'VIP care').

Among others who chose private hospitals when they were infected with the COVID-19 virus were Karnataka Chief Minister BS Yediyurappa; Tamil Nadu Governor Banwarilal Purohit; Tamil Nadu's electricity minister P. Thangamani, higher education Minister K.P. Anbalagan and cooperation minister Sellur K Raju; Punjab's rural development minister Tript Singh Bajwa and the Madhya Pradesh chief minister Shivraj Singh Chouhan. The few 'VIPs' who deigned to use the facilities of public hospitals treated these as fiefdoms. A senior doctor in a leading public hospital spoke to me of a member of Parliament who insisted on having his personal 'servant' at call while he recuperated from COVID in his VIP hospital room. The young man was made to sleep on a bed in the neighbouring COVID ward. Terrified of catching the dreaded infection, he tried to run away. The MP traced him to the railway station, and sent the police to catch him and bring him back to the hospital. The doctor told me that such COVID-slaves were not unusual.

*

There were many models that India could have followed, or at least learned from, but did not.

The strategy of South Korea was 'Test, Trace and Cure', unlike India's, which could be described as 'Trace, Test and Cure'. South Korea never went in for a lockdown. By the time the WHO issued its recommendation in mid-March for countries to 'test, test, test', South Korea had spent weeks doing precisely that, quickly developing the capability to test an average of 12,000 people—and sometimes as many as 20,000—a day at hundreds of drive-through and walk-in testing centres. These mobile centres conducted the tests free of charge within 10 minutes, and the results were sent to people's phones within 24 hours. By mid-March more than 270,000 people had been tested.[262] India, with a population of 1.3 billion against South Korea's 50 million, was, as we have seen, conducting less than 100,000 tests a day even two months after the WHO recommendation.

But there were models even within the country, which the union government chose not to follow. Apart from the stellar work done by the Kerala government in responding at the early stages of the pandemic and building vibrant community support for its interventions which succeeded in controlling the surge of the epidemic in the state, one of the most significant examples is the remarkable turnaround in India's biggest slum, Dharavi in Mumbai. Nearly ten lakh—a million—people live in this fabled slum spread over an area of just 2.1 square kilometres. After Dharavi registered its first positive case on 1st April, most observers feared it would become a site of massive, even runaway deaths. The COVID-19 virus spreads most in unsanitary, densely populated places, and with 277,136 persons per square kilometre, Dharavi is one of the world's most densely populated areas. Often a dozen people live in a single room, and community toilets are shared by literally hundreds of people. The slum is pock-marked with open drains and broken sewers, and few people have piped water supply. All of this spelt almost certain disaster for this thriving nucleus of the mega city's informal economy, with innumerable small units of pottery, leather products and accessories. A number of its residents are also factory workers and domestic workers.

Remarkably, Dharavi managed to avert disaster. It relied on a policy of intensive screening, testing, isolation and community participation, offering another inspiring contrast to a blunt sledgehammer lockdown. None of the three national strategies for fighting COVID—lockdown, physical distancing and hand hygiene—had any chance of success in Dharavi. Home isolation was also impossible. Still, by mid-June, Dharavi was way ahead of most of the rest of the country in flattening the infection curve. By 12 June, its daily growth rate was 1.57%, just half of the Mumbai rate of 3%; and its doubling rate was 44 days, against 22 days for the rest of the city.[263]

What explains this extraordinary success? Public health officials first undertook massive screening for COVID symptoms, first house to house, and then in a network of centres, including dispensaries, run by 350 private health providers. The screening was followed by early quarantining in community-created large and friendly quarantine and isolation centres in places like schools, wedding halls and sports complexes. A new community-based 200-bed field hospital was also established in record time.[264] To engage and bolster the morale of those in quarantine and isolation, 'laughter yoga' and entertainment were organized. There was also a massive drive to clean and maintain the community toilets.[265] This is all it took. Not an authoritarian top-down lockdown with its unconscionable exclusions and immense human costs, but a highly localized, community-based policy of massive screening and early quarantining in friendly, respectful spaces and a dedicated field hospital.

*

While we must hold the Indian government culpable for its disastrous policies, the pandemic has also revealed the limitations of science itself.

These limitations became obvious to me several times as the pandemic spread across the planet. For instance, when the Delhi government announced the result of its serological survey that 23% of Delhi's population had been infected by the virus by June end and 28% by mid-August, I made a quick back-of-the-envelope calculation about the number of deaths we should have had if we accept the predicted mortality rates that the government chose at first to believe. I came to a stunning figure of 1.5 lakh to 2 lakh deaths. I don't have much faith in my mathematical skills, so I checked with some public-health experts. They concurred with my calculations.

This led me into immense bewilderment. The official death count on 15 June was 1500 in Delhi. Scientists say that the official death count anywhere in India could be wrong by a ratio of at least 10. Even that would mean 15,000 deaths, not 1.5 lakh. I came to two conclusions. Either scientists had been dangerously wrong in their projections, or that tens of thousands of people were dying and none of this was being recorded.

I asked a number of public health experts whom I respect how they would understand this massive gap. Public-health expert Vikas Bajpai responded to me very thoughtfully. 'First of all, the projected numbers, which are scary if true, are not a matter of our insistence,' he said. 'They follow from the statistics put out by the government and other agencies. I feel that the government should be made to account for something that is the culmination of its own findings. It cannot be allowed to use data and statistics as per its convenience—use them when it suits its convenience and rubbish them when it does not. Why it is, what it is, cannot be a matter of conjecture or happy assumptions; it ought to be reasoned out scientifically. So, our insistence is nothing beyond stating that if the results of the survey are true then this is what follows. Its denial or confirmation ought to be a matter of scientific investigation.'

He then responded to the human part of my dilemma—the terrible effect on the poor of the draconian lockdown that had been justified as a measure necessary to prevent the massive deaths predicted by scientists who appeared to be advising the government. 'As a guiding principle, I would insist that in order to be perceptive of and be able to register the agony of the poorest of the poor, we always need to be willing to err on the side of caution, for the well to do shall always manage to have their agony taken note of and cared for. Would you and I have been convinced of the possibility of the prevailing mayhem had we been told of it say sometime in December or January? Would we have believed in January first week that India is soon going to witness a migration of hungry and harassed people which might even exceed that of 1947; that we could be staring at unemployment rates of 40 to 45 per cent; or that India's economy shall contract by almost 9 per cent? We may perhaps have not believed this even during the initial phase of the pandemic, yet all of this has come true.'

Vikram Patel, professor of Global Health at Harvard, a scientist himself, believes that scientists 'failed in [the] obligation to acknowledge the uncertainties in our observations, the limitations of our methods and the importance of other traditions of knowledge'. In his introspective meditation with great moral salience, he speaks of the pandemic being 'littered with premature, and often inaccurate, scientific predictions ranging from the estimates of the numbers of people who will die unless nations impose a lockdown to the effectiveness of drug treatments'. He is particularly critical of the scientific discipline of modelling, because 'it was its estimates of mountains of dead bodies which fuelled the panic and led to the unprecedented restrictions on public life around the world'. These models never 'explicitly acknowledged the huge assumptions that were made, for example that mortality was distributed evenly across the population (incorrect, because it is heavily concentrated in the elderly) or that everyone who is not infected is vulnerable (likely to be incorrect as evidence of innate immunity mounts)'.[266]

Patel says that it is not surprising that some scientists vociferously called for governments to act swiftly to impose lockdowns. 'After all, most of my community, and the government officials who conjure and implement these policies, enjoy salaried jobs which can seamlessly pivot to online platforms which we can operate with ease from our spacious homes in which being locked down can evolve into a rather congenial opportunity to master culinary skills and not have to commute to work…The fact that many lives will be lost as a result of the lockdowns is now emerging across the world…Most of these deaths will occur in the poorest communities.'[267]

It is clear to me that not just the public officials who took horrific decisions, but the scientists who called for punishing lockdowns need to take moral responsibility for the intense suffering their recommendations have resulted in. But it is striking that none of the hardliner scientists who advocated a total lockdown for India have found it necessary to explain why the cataclysm of mountains of bodies which they predicted has not occurred; why death tolls remain much, much lower than their estimates even months after the unlocking. A more sober assessment of the risks of the contagion by them may have led to a more sober choice of policy strategies and so much devastation could have been avoided.

*

Postscript

The Indian Public Health Association (IPHA), Indian Association of Preventive and Social Medicine (IAPSM) and Indian Association of Epidemiologists (IAE) Joint

COVID-19 Task Force wrote to the prime minister on 25 May 2020.[268] In a dire indictment of the government's handling of the pandemic, they wrote, India's draconian lockdown 'is presumably in response to a modelling exercise from an influential institution which was a "worst-case simulation". The model had come up with an estimated 2.2 million deaths globally. Subsequent events have proved that the predictions of this model were way off the mark.' They continued: 'Had the Government of India consulted epidemiologists who had better grasp of disease transmission dynamics compared to modellers, it would have perhaps been better served. From the limited information available in the public domain, it seems that the government was primarily advised by clinicians and academic epidemiologists with limited field training and skills. Policy makers apparently relied overwhelmingly on general administrative bureaucrats. The engagement with expert technocrats in the areas of epidemiology, public health, preventive medicine and social scientists was limited. India is paying a heavy price both in terms of humanitarian crisis and disease spread. The incoherent and often rapidly shifting strategies and policies, especially at the national level, are more a reflection of "afterthought" and "catching up" phenomenon on part of the policy makers rather than a well thought cogent strategy with an epidemiologic basis.'[269]

By the end of August, India's officially acknowledged figure for COVID-19 cases was 35 lakh, or 3.5 million, and it was adding more new cases than any other country in the world. Dr Ashish Jha of Harvard explained to Karan Thapar that our high positivity rate was a clue that we were testing too little and missing very large numbers of positive cases. Our positivity rate at the end of August was still around 8-9%. This means that out of 10 or 11 cases tested, one turns out to be positive. New York, one of the worst-hit cities in the world now has a positivity rate of around 1%, and South Korea even less than 1%. What this means is that for a 100 people being tested you find one positive case in these locations. This is why scientists estimate that for every case that India is identifying, there could be 5, 10 or even 20 which we could be missing. This is also reflected in the serological studies that have been done in Delhi and Mumbai. This means that by the end of August India's actual case burden may have been at least 70 million (seven crore) or perhaps even 700 million (70 crore). [270]

By the end of August, we saw the infection gradually moving away from the big metropolises into the countryside. Because these habitations are less dense, the disease would spread more slowly. But the broken health systems in these locations would cancel out the benefits of less crowding. As Dr Jha said, the wages of continuous conscious under-investment in public health will be borne most by the poor. The poor will suffer also because of hubris, the hubris of the leadership of the country which chose to take decisions to deal with the pandemic without consulting with scientific opinion, but also the unrepentant hubris of segments of the scientific community which predicted doomsday outcomes which turned out to be spectacularly alarmist and resulted in a sledgehammer strategy to protect only the privileged and bring immense suffering upon the poor.

11

The Path Not Taken

The world has battled many health emergencies and killer pandemics in the past, but never before has the instrument of a drastic lockdown of large populations been used as the principal preventive public health strategy. Even this time round, no government anywhere in the world chose to do to its people what the Indian government did. It is true that many other countries also adopted the strategy of lockdowns as infections crossed national borders and deaths were reported. A fifth of the populations of the world came under lockdown.[271] But nowhere was the strategy as callously and ruthlessly implemented as in India. Researchers from the Blavatnik School of Government at the University of Oxford created an 'Oxford COVID-19 Government Response Tracker' to document responses of governments worldwide to the pandemic and aggregated the scores into a 'Stringency Index'.[272] They rated India's lockdown as the most stringent in the world, with measures like 'school closures, border closures, travel bans, etc.'

There are many fierce critics, in India as in many parts of the word, of the strategy of the lockdown. A few among them believe that some form of lockdown was necessary in India to save thousands of lives, but regard the planning, execution and use of the window for public health preparation as abysmal, resulting in the crisis in which we find ourselves.

But there are others, and this writer is one of them, who believe that the policy of a stringent lockdown was dangerously wrong in principle itself. The lockdown was disastrous public-health, disastrous economics, disastrous sociology, and unconscionable public ethics. It was, as argued in detail in earlier chapters, unforgivable for a country with enormous historically embedded economic and social inequalities. My fundamental objection to the policy of the lockdown in India is that it could never—even in its best implementation—have ensured safety from infection for the large mass of the poor, and yet the government went ahead with it. The living conditions of the poor excluded them from the possibility of any kind of effective physical distancing. And since the COVID-19 virus, like any virus, loves crowded indoor spaces packed with human bodies with low immunity, it is most likely to infect the labouring poor. When that happens, the consistently under-resourced, broken public health system would be unable to test, treat and cure the majority of the poor. Had the Indian government not realised this?

I can do no better than to quote medical anthropologist Carlo Caduff.[273] He describes the strategy of lockdown as 'massive and unprecedented', and finds it 'stunning' that 'extreme measures that affect billions of people and that push societies to the edge of collapse, creating poverty, hunger, misery, debt, and unemployment' were taken 'without any serious consideration of the social, political and economic consequences'. The response, Caduff points out, was cast into the language and ideology of 'nationalism', suggesting a common and equal threat across the population. It demanded 'equal sacrifice'. This obscured the central reality that the contagion 'disproportionately affected the already vulnerable, along lines of age and race…[and] poor and marginalized people'. He could have added persons with disabilities. These tendencies were nurtured by a 'growing sense of panic, constant media sensationalism, deep authoritarian longings… misleading mortality calculations and, most importantly, a trust in the power of mathematical disease modelling'. 'A virus causes disease, not hunger and unemployment,' Caduff concludes powerfully. 'It is not the pandemic but the response to it that threatens the livelihood of millions of people.'

In India, with the strategy of the lockdown, and that too with a perfunctory minimalist relief package, the state drew clear lines between those who were to be saved, and those who could be sacrificed; those whose lives mattered, and those who were expendable.

India, China and Pakistan in Another War—Against COVID

We have seen that even after the world's harshest lockdown that lasted more than 60 days, the curve of COVID-19 infections did not flatten in India.[274] The massive gaps in the country's health infrastructure remained. By early September, five months after the lockdown was announced, India had hit the highest daily rate of new identified COVID-19 cases in the world, fast approaching one lakh cases a day. It also became the country with the second highest number of identified cases, after the United States.

It is apparent that the policies of the union government

to battle the COVID-19 pandemic have failed. But some people suggest that for a country of the size and complexity of India, it is doing the best it can. After all, they argue, the pandemic has even brought the most powerful country in the world to its knees. They suggest that comparisons with the successes of countries like New Zealand and South Korea are inappropriate. These are small countries. India is much larger, much more complex, much harder to govern.

So let us contrast India with the two countries with which it is most often hyphenated: China and Pakistan. The infection originated in China, and it was the first country to deploy the instrument of the lockdown. But even at the peak of the pandemic, China, with its powerful and notoriously authoritarian state apparatus, used the harsh instrument of a sweeping lockdown mainly in its large cities, restricting the movement of just 56 million people, or around 5% of its population of 1.4 billion people.[275] India, which prides itself as a democracy, imposed at one stroke a complete lockdown on its entire population of 1.3 billion, and that too with a notice of three and a half hours.

China succeeded in arresting the total number of identified infections to around 85,000 (and deaths to around 4,600, many of these in the early stages in Wuhan). Let me underline this: the cumulative number of infections in China from the start of the pandemic until September is less than the number of *new* infections India was adding *every day* from early September. Moreover, by mid-May, China was able to reopen schools and universities. Travel was restricted only for travellers from other countries which were COVID-infection hot-spots. And to add to all of this, China is one of the few countries which have been able to sustain a positive rate of economic growth (at around 3.5%).

The success in China is attributed to many factors by experts. China went in for early but restricted lockdowns. It activated the strong network of neighbourhood and village committees from its communist past for aggressive contact tracing, quarantine and isolation. It was also aided by a much stronger public health infrastructure than India's. In addition, a popular scientific attitude was encouraged by the Chinese leadership, in contrast to India where the political leadership politicised the spread of the virus by blaming it on specific communities, and promoted unscientific claims and remedies.

The contrast with Pakistan would be even more damaging to India's self-image. India has 2.3 times more cases per million population than Pakistan, and the infection curve there is declining, unlike in India. And this, when Pakistan has a lower per capita income, an equally broken health-care system and large populations similarly living in cramped and unhygienic shanties. (Sri Lanka, with a more robust public health system, has 21.5 times *less* cases than India).

Experts believe that Pakistan benefited, ironically, because it refused to go in for a stringent lockdown. At the time that India went in for its lockdown, the Pakistani prime minister, Imran Khan, declared that if Pakistan was an industrialized country like Italy, France or the United States, he would have imposed a complete lockdown. But in Pakistan, he observed, 25% of the people are under the poverty line. 'They can't afford even two square meals a day. If working-class Pakistanis are locked up for two weeks, how will they feed their families?'[276]

A certain breed of Indians who regard themselves as 'nationalist' will hate me for saying this, but the 'playboy', 'elite' Imran Khan displayed much greater sensitivity and compassion for his working-class fellow country-people than Narendra Modi, whose political calling card is his 'humble origins'. And it is this concern for the working poor that saved Pakistan both from a surge in infections and a severe economic downturn. Pakistani economist Altaf Khan explains that because there was a lax lockdown in Pakistan, most people continued to find work in the cities and very few moved out into the countryside. [277] In India, the shock-and-awe lockdown first trapped the working people in slum shanties, without food and employment, where the dense and unsanitary living conditions—in addition to the crush of long lines to collect charity food—aggravated the spread of the virus. And then, as they returned to their villages amidst immense and entirely avoidable suffering, they inadvertently carried the virus to those far corners of the country where even elementary public health services are often unavailable.

The COVID-19 pandemic was to a degree an 'act of god', as the country's finance minister maintains. But the cruel lockdown and a relief package of less than 2% of GDP (contrasting with 13.2% in the US, 7% in China, 11.8% in Brazil and 20% in Japan[278]) were conscious public policy choices. As India stares at a bleak future of a more extended period of runaway infection than perhaps anywhere else on earth and of years of mass hunger and joblessness, the man elected to govern the country posts photographs of himself feeding peacocks and reading a newspaper as ducks walk by in his spacious green garden. He spends scarce public resources in a grandiose plan to build a new parliament, central secretariat complex and prime minister's residence. He grows and grooms a beard modelled on rishis of calendar art and religious soap operas, and lays the foundation of a grand temple to be built at the site of a violent, illegal demolition. The catastrophe that we find ourselves in is the direct outcome of such leadership of hubris and narcissism, with an almost pathological absence of compassion.

What Could the Government Have Done Differently?

Let me return to my question: what could India have done differently? The stark answer is, virtually everything.

We must begin with the first and central decision—imposing a nationwide lockdown, that too without notice or preparation. We have seen that had the government consulted widely with public-health experts, epidemiologists, economists, social scientists, and studied the global experience carefully—indeed, listened carefully and respectfully to scientists even *within* the establishment—it would have ruled out lockdown as bad public health, because you cannot save millions of working people from infection by pushing them into mass hunger. It should also have been ruled out as immoral. In a country in which the large majority live in crowded tenements without water or sanitation, a policy of enforcing physical distancing and radical hygiene extended protection only to the privileged and relatively privileged people and unleashed immense suffering on the poor, and put them at greater risk of infection. We could have instead followed the examples of countries like South Korea, with a focus on extensive testing, public education and limited containment.

But even if parts of the country with high infection were locked down, the government could have first explained the reasons for this to the people, addressing most of all the working poor. It could, with scientists and economists, have responded to questions in open, regular and empathetic press briefings. For the period of limited and localised lockdowns, it could have ensured that every household would receive unconditional cash transfers of 7000 rupees per household and, through a universal public distribution system, would also receive essential food rations, including pulses and oil. Economists Prabhat Patnaik and Jayati Ghosh have calculated that for three and six months, respectively, for all Indians, this would have cost not more than 3% of GDP, and a manageable depletion of India's food grain stocks of 7.7 crore tonnes.[279]

The government could have arranged repayment of loan instalments of SMSEs for six months to ensure they do not sink. A cornerstone of its revival strategy could have been massive public spending for a greatly expanded employment guarantee programme, extending it to urban India as well. Older people are most at risk; the government could have pegged pensions at half the minimum wage, universalised these, and ensured that during the pandemic these would be hand-delivered to older persons so as to not place them at risk.

Migrants, and other citizens, could have been given at least a couple of weeks to return to their homes before even a limited lockdown was enforced. The government could have ensured full passenger train operations and reserved all seats for a week for free travel of migrants on a first-come-first-served basis. It had every capacity to accomplish this, but was bereft of the will and sense of public duty required to do so. In normal times, the railways run 13,452 passenger trains, transporting 2.3 crore (23 million) passengers daily.[280] Yet in over a month and a half after it belatedly started Shramik (workers') trains, it transported less than 60 lakh (6 million) workers.[281]

The government could have ensured free water tankers supplied water in slum shanties throughout the day until the pandemic ebbs, to enable people to wash their hands regularly and secure personal hygiene.

It could have massively ramped up helplines for both mental health and domestic violence assistance, as well as mental health OPDs and places of safety for battered women. It could have emptied custodial beggar homes, women's homes and children's homes for those in conflict with the law, and offered instead voluntary and dignified places of safety for all at-risk persons. To make our overcrowded prisons safer, it could have used this moment to do what the Supreme Court has directed for decades: to grant bail to or discharge all under-trial prisoners except perhaps those with the most serious charges. Even among these, those who are older than 65 and therefore at special risk, could have been given bail for the period of the pandemic. The government could have discharged all people held for petty offences.

It would have been impossible to overnight rebuild the public health system, broken for decades. But the government could, like in Spain, have deployed all personnel, beds and equipment of private hospitals for public use, free of cost, for the duration of the pandemic. It could by ordinance have ordered that no patient be turned away or charged by any private hospital for diagnosis or treatment of symptoms which could be of the Coronavirus. It could have also ensured that treatment of all other ailments did not suffer during the pandemic. Beds for COVID-19 patients should not have been created by snatching away beds from patients suffering from other ailments. The government could have instead converted several stadiums, universities and hotels into COVID hospitals temporarily from the start. The Delhi government belatedly, after the lockdown was over, responded to the massive shortage of isolation and treatment beds for patients with mild to moderate symptoms by temporarily acquiring the campus of a well-resourced religious trust to create a 15000-bed facility, akin to the community hospitals created in China. I have friends who were referred to this facility, and they found it airy, clean and therapeutic. This is not rocket-science; establishing such large sites for post-disaster relief is something IAS officers are routinely trained for. I am baffled why this was not done in the first couple of weeks across India by district magistrates; and none of this required any lockdown, as infection rates at that time in most of the country were very low. The government could have guaranteed that every person, regardless of class, would be entitled to the same quality of quarantine facilities. London moved homeless persons to all vacant hotel beds for the duration of the lockdown, even luxury hotels, paid for by the state. There was no reason why India could not have done the same.

The government could, from the start, have incentivised public and private corporations to exponentially expand production of PPEs, testing kits, ventilators and medicinal oxygen. Most front-line health workers, like ASHA and ICDS workers and sanitation workers, are grossly underpaid and lack job security. They could have been regularised as government servants, to remedy the injustice with which they have been forced to work so far and bolster their morale at a time when they were going to risk their lives to save the lives of others.

You may ask, where would the money come from? Most countries which went down the road of lockdown invested 10 to 20% of GDP in public spending to prevent massive hunger and unemployment.[282] India's additional public spending turned out to be less than 1% in the first stage, and less than 2% even several months into the pandemic. The government could also have imposed a cess of 2% on the wealth of just the top 1%, and an inheritance tax of 33%. This would have raised all the resources we need for everything I have suggested here.

Were we ever likely to do any of this? The clear answer is no. But not because this was not feasible. It was. Other countries have done all of this, and much more. It did not happen because the government and people of privilege did not allow this to happen. We cannot blame the COVID virus for the humanitarian crisis which has engulfed us, growing into probably the worst we will witness during our lives. We must blame only ourselves.

12

In Conclusion: A Moment for Civilizational Introspection

Defence Colony is one of Delhi's affluent, leafy neighbourhoods, centrally located, with wide roads, parks and many popular restaurants. Early into the lockdown, tragedy hit one of its plush apartment blocks. A couple in their 80s and their son tested positive for COVID-19. The elderly man tragically died in hospital, his wife was discharged, and his son fought for his life for a long time on a ventilator. Fortunately, he survived. At one point during this time of trial, a person from the family thought it fit to call the local police to complain about their security guard. Their security guard was Muslim. That was reason enough for them to surmise that he had secretly participated in the Tablighi Jamaat congregation in Nizamuddin. They were certain that it was he who had brought the infection into their home.

The Delhi Police acted promptly on their complaint, registering a criminal case under Sections 188, 269 and 270 of the Indian Penal Code against the guard, charging him with committing a 'negligent malignant act likely to spread infection of disease dangerous to life'. They also issued an advisory to the residents of Defence Colony to be careful of their domestic helpers who might bring the infection into their homes. The matter was widely reported in the press, and there was widespread rage among readers and television viewers over the criminal irresponsibility of the security guard. The guard was initially reported by the police to be missing. They however quickly caught the 'fugitive' and sent him to be tested for COVID-19. He turned out to be negative.

It was later revealed that the grandson of the Defence Colony household studied abroad and had returned before the lockdown by an international flight. From details that emerged later, it appeared that it was not the guard who had irresponsibly endangered the family but members of the family who had probably put *him* in danger by asking him to run errands for them in violation of the strict lockdown of the early weeks.

The police never satisfactorily explained why they filed a criminal case against the hapless guard. No one thought it fit to apologize to him. No one thought it fit to charge the family for violating curfew rules because, after all, middle-class families in India find it difficult to manage their lives without domestic help. No one thought it fit to charge them with endangering the life of the security guard.

The story did not end there. Some weeks later, the same family employed an 18-year-old domestic helper. They arranged to get her tested for COVID-19. Three days later, the report came in. She had tested positive. It was 10 at night. The family turned her out of the apartment. She was distraught and began to wail in the dark and empty streets, not knowing where she should go, and how, at this hour in the curfew of the lockdown. Some other residents came out of their homes to enquire when they heard her crying. The security guards also gathered around her. Among them was a doctor, who gave her a PPE kit. Someone called for an ambulance, others called up her male relative. One ambulance arrived, but refused to carry a person who was COVID-positive. Three hours later, a second ambulance finally took the frightened girl to hospital.[283]

Writer Arundhati Roy, in a conversation with Karwan-e-Mohabbat, said that COVID-19 is a virus but it is also an X-ray, an X-ray which has exposed 'this desolation that we call civilization, this greed that we call happiness, this horrifying injustice that we call "business as usual"[.]'[284]

The traumatic months of lockdown have indeed laid bare our broken society, the near-complete estrangement of people of privilege from the working poor in India. These months have revealed ruling and 'aspirational' classes entirely and effortlessly accepting of—indeed, stunningly comfortable with—great inequality; people bereft of elementary empathy and solidarity. They have confirmed that the veneer of modernity and the progressive, egalitarian values of the constitution remain, in the prophetic words of Babasaheb Ambedkar, no deeper than a coat of paint.

In my book *Looking Away: Inequality, Prejudice and Indifference in New India*, I examined why and how the bulk of India's rich and middle classes are among the most uncaring in the world, mired still in the cruelties of caste and class, with a singular capacity to look at injustice and suffering and simply turn away. I wrote of the exile of the poor from our conscience and our consciousness. The lockdown has shown precisely how absolute and brutal this exile is.

For most young people growing up in middle-class homes, the poor are visible at every turn, but only in their instrumentality as labour who exist to service their every need. They never know them as classmates, as colleagues or competitors at work, or as friends in a playground or cinema theatre. They see them as problems, or as troubling realities that ruin their peace of mind. They fail to recognize that the working poor inhabit shanties only because the state does not invest in social housing, and that the middle-classes enjoy three times more subsidies than the poor, and the super-rich are given astronomically higher subsidies. (Until a few years ago, every union government budget would contain a line called 'revenues foregone', or tax exemptions and tax holidays for industry, which would be around five lakh crore rupees, enough to provide decent education or health care to all.) Rich and middle-class Indians also see the urban poor as vaguely dangerous—who will cheat, burgle or kill their rich employers. Underclass men, especially, are feared as potential rapists.

When the COVID-19 infection hit us, the working poor were seen as dangerous in new ways, this time as potential carriers and spreaders of the infection. We wanted them suddenly at bay. We ignored science which would have demonstrated that it was not the poor who endangered us, but we who endangered the poor when they came into contact with us. After all, it was people who could afford international flight tickets who brought the virus into India, often Club Class.

My colleagues involved in food relief in several cities in the country reported that many households refused to pay domestic workers during the lockdown. Gated colonies placed multiple restrictions on them even after the lockdown was partially lifted, and immediately blamed them if anyone in the employers' households was infected. In one instance, a public notice was issued to not allow domestic helpers to touch lift buttons ('her hands may be infected'). I was speaking with members of a domestic workers' union in Jaipur. They said that they had fought for ten years against humiliating practices of what they called 'untouchability' in the homes they worked in, such as separate vessels for eating and drinking and restrictions on their using the same toilets as their employers. But they said the pandemic had reversed all of these gains, and the untouchability they now had to endure was even worse than a decade earlier. The restrictions of a health emergency mirrored age-old prejudices and the apartheid of class and caste, and everyone was comfortable with this.

We welcomed the strategy of a nationwide lockdown—the most draconian and the largest in the world, it must be repeated, with the smallest relief package. We felt safe inside our homes. Mostly deprived of domestic help, we were inconvenienced, but adjusted willingly for our own safety. We also adjusted to working from home, secure that our salaries and savings and health insurance would see us through. We celebrated the cleaner air and birdsong. We grappled with boredom and occasional depression, but it was a time also to rebuild our bonds with our families, and there were the endless pleasures of online entertainment.

Through all of this we were indifferent to the reality outside our safe homes, that the lockdown fell like a meteor on the lives of millions of the working poor. They had difficult but fully functional lives before the lockdown, built mostly without state support. After possibly some years—if any at all—in poorly resourced schools, they travelled far to escape the dead-end poverty and caste oppression of the countryside. The cities were uniformly unwelcoming to them. The state made no arrangements for even the most basic, affordable housing, or to protect their rights as workers. Instead it was consistently hostile to them, rendering illegal and demolishing their slum shanties or roadside vending stalls. Still they survived and struggled on, working to build, clean and sustain the cities, and improve the lives of their families.

The lockdown by design had nothing to offer them except to destroy overnight the lives they had built for themselves. The safety of physical distancing and hand-washing was impossible for them. With their livelihoods carpet-bombed by state policy, they were suddenly forced to endure the very hunger from which they escaped when they had moved to the city. And now when they sought to return to the solace of their homes in their villages and the company of people they could call their own, the state unleashed its police force to stop them, thrash them, and douse them in harmful disinfectants. Or it let them exhaust themselves to near-death trekking on blazing highways. Despite this, we in the middle-classes readily demonstrated our support for the lockdown, cheerily banging utensils or lighting candles, as instructed by the prime minister.

It is sobering that most of the migrants trudging or cycling home in dangerous journeys, dying on railway tracks or of hunger and exhaustion on trains without food and water, were between 15 and 30 years old. But for the accident of their birth, they could have been in high school or university, studying online, or working from the safety of their homes, fighting tedium with an overdose of Netflix.

The brazen class bias of state policies did not trouble us at all. All government servants and most employees in the formal private sector were assured full salaries during the lockdown, or salaries with bearable cuts. The poor lost their livelihoods and had to make do with financial handouts amounting to no more than two days' wages (500 rupees a month paid to those with Jan Dhan accounts was less than two days' statutory minimum wages), a non-enforced and non-enforceable 'appeal' from the prime minister to their employers to pay them wages, and charity meals—often just gruel—for which they had to queue up for hours like beggars each day. All of this seemed in the fitness of things to us; the poor have survived worse conditions than this, after all, they are used to this, so this wasn't too bad. It seemed also in the fitness of things that while we could quarantine in the comfort of our homes or in hired hotel rooms, the poor who attempted to get to safer places of refuge than their rented hovels in the cities were forced into crowded dormitories in which physical distancing was an impossibility, with clogged bathrooms, inedible food and disrespectful staff.

Governments and business did not help them both because they did not care and because they did not want them to move. They did not see these workers as human beings of equal humanity. If they had, there would have been special buses and flights for them, too, as there were for Indian professionals or tourists stranded overseas, and middle-class students in hostels in Kota and elsewhere. In fact, as we have seen, when the government did belatedly start a limited number of trains for migrants, for the lottery of getting a seat on these trains the workers had to negotiate a complicated maze of bureaucratic requirements—apply online, get a health certificate, a no-objection certificate and then go into quarantine at the other end. But when the union government decided to restore domestic flights, the minister in charge announced that people would not be required to furnish health certificates before they travel, or be quarantined in their destinations, because this was not 'practical'. What was not practical for resourced and networked air-travellers was made mandatory for pauperised workers without social capital.

The foundational postulate of the Declaration of Philadelphia in 1919 that marked the birth of the International Labour Organization declared more than 100 years ago that 'labour is not a commodity' and that 'all human beings, irrespective of race, creed or sex, have a right to pursue both their material well-being and their spiritual development in conditions of freedom and dignity, of economic security and equal opportunity'.[285] We failed, even these 100 years later, to see workers in anything of the fullness of their agency and humanness. We still saw them only instrumentally as a factor of production—labour which should be obediently available on call whenever big businesses were able to restart their enterprises.

This should be a moment of civilizational introspection, a recognition of the collapse of our moral centre as a nation and as a people. In coming months and years, as so many crises converge in a confluence, as hunger spreads like a cancer and jobs crumble due to an enfeebled economy, children are pulled out of school, women endure violence, loneliness grows into another silent pandemic, and the long-term impact of the criminal neglect of public health programmes begins to show in needless suffering and deaths, will we at last learn lessons of solidarity, equality and justice?

*

There is no better time to recall the talisman Mahatma Gandhi left for us. When in doubt and confusion, he counselled in a letter he typed just months before he was killed, think of the most vulnerable person you know, and ask if the measures will improve her life and freedom. The measures the state has opted for during the pandemic may arguably protect you and me, but they have wrought havoc on this 'last person' whom Gandhiji had asked us to remember before we took any step. If policy-makers had held to their hearts the talisman which the father of our nation left for us, they could never have opted for a lockdown that destroyed in one fell blow her livelihood, her already tenuous support structures, her dignity, her trust and her hope. The arrogance and casual cruelty of the Indian state in imposing a sudden, complete

and devastating lockdown is a crime against the people of India. It is, and must be recognized to be, a crime against humanity.

Since the early days of the pandemic, a metaphor we heard very often was of war. Health professionals, governments and people the world over were fighting a war, indeed a world war, against a virus which threatens to destroy tens of thousands of lives, and, as some believe, even the world as we know it. Every war has weapons. Some weapons were obvious in waging this war—science; health personnel, equipment and infrastructure; public investments; state capacities; and the quality of political leadership. But what would be most decisive if we were to emerge victorious was a weapon rarely remembered, understood or nurtured. This was our solidarity. This is not a war. It is a struggle, in which solidarity alone between classes and genders, between nations, and between people will enable us to overcome. We can only overcome together.

Solidarity is many things. It is my capacity to feel your pain as my own. It is my incapacity to look away when you suffer. It is kindness. It is collective struggle. It is the moral resolve that we must take care of each other.

There were indeed many extraordinary displays of solidarity in our country amidst the trauma of the pandemic and lockdown. Most of all by public health professionals at all levels. Often badly let down by a state which has not invested nearly enough in their protection, nor in testing kits, equipment and infrastructure, they still battled at the frontlines of this war. Unmindful of their own safety, cut off from or risking the lives of their loved ones, they fought to save our lives.

And then there were what I call 'circles of kindness.' Each time I was on the streets helping distribute food to the homeless and destitute, I was edified by the numbers of ordinary people reaching out to the hungry with food and care. The police mostly did not stop them, even if they had no formal permission. I even heard reports of police persons themselves organizing food kitchens for the hungry at some police stations.

In Nizamuddin, I asked a homeless man how he was surviving. He said he had just a little money saved up when the lockdown was imposed, which he was spending on food. But not just for his own family. He also fed three other families which slept on the pavement beside him. He was not related to them in any way. But how could he eat, he explained to me, and watch their children sleep hungry? In a lane in Old Delhi, I spotted a cycle-rickshaw cart piled with packets of roti and sabzi. The owner of a modest tent-house, I was told, would get 500 meals cooked every morning and distribute these to people rendered destitute by the lockdown. In Ghazipur, during the long march of migrants on the highway out of Delhi, I found many people driving up in their cars packed with drinking water pouches and food, which they handed out to grateful migrants abandoned by the state.

There were many young people in cities and towns who were defying their families by setting out each morning to distribute food to the hungry. Some slept in separate rooms from the rest of their families; others moved out of their homes to their offices, to save their families from infection. My young colleagues in the Karwan-e-Mohabbat project resolved to drive out to distribute cooked food and dry rations from the second day of the lockdown to the homeless who they knew would be worst hit. We organized masks and gloves, but the risk of infection always remained. 'I'm frightened of Corona,' one young volunteer told me. 'But their suffering is greater than my fear.'

Rohit Kumar, educator and writer, describes many such acts of both resilience and kindness during the lockdown. He speaks of what another educator, Parker Palmer, calls 'the tragic gap'—the gap between the way we know things can be and the way they actually are. He explains that 'in the face of overwhelming problems, we tend to flip either into the realm of corrosive cynicism and stop believing that anything will change and end up living only for ourselves, or we flip into the world of irrelevant idealism and empty optimism, and "float above it all". The result is the same, as both the cynics and so-called idealists end up doing little good in the world…Palmer tells us that very few choose to stand in the tragic gap because they know that doing so will break their hearts. But the key, he says, is to let the pain and tragedy break our hearts open and let empathy flow, instead of letting them shatter like exploding grenades, spewing shards of hatred and anger out into the world. Those who choose to stand in the tragic gap understand full well that they will not be able to solve the great problems of the world, but they also understand they have a responsibility to be a part of the solutions, however small. And in these, the most trying times in recent modern history, that is enough.'[286]

And yet, this period has also witnessed the most profound decimation of our solidarities. Let us play a mind game. Suppose all of us of the middle-class in formal sector employment were informed after the precipitous lockdown that none of us would be assured any salary for the period of the lockdown—that, instead, the state would endeavour to pay some of us maybe two days' wages and give us six kilos of grain. Suppose we had little in our banks to fall back on. Suppose we were also without any kind of health insurance and could only depend on ramshackle public health systems. Suppose we had no running water or toilets in our homes. Would we then have accepted being locked into our homes as a reasonable and acceptable response to the pandemic?

In a survey undertaken during the lockdown by my colleagues in the Centre for Equity Studies, 97% of the workers we interviewed testified to not receiving their wages during the lockdown. The overwhelming majority of the salaried middle-class did. Solidarity demanded that we in the middle-class should have been outraged that the poor were cruelly stranded overnight without work and wages, unlike us. We should have demanded from the state that every worker in the informal sector be paid for the entire duration of the lockdown, no different from us, at least the statutory minimum wage, and that the state should ensure this payment if employers failed to. But we did not.

Let us play another mind game. Suppose you worked far from the place you call home, living in sub-standard, overcrowded rooms or tenements on rent, and suddenly you were left without food and work, terrified also by a disease that had brought the world to its knees and could kill you and your loved ones. Would you still obediently stay on in the city, ready to die among strangers, watching your children die? Or would you desperately do anything, anything to reach your loved ones—and the only place you can call your own home—even if this meant walking hundreds of kilometres, dodging a hostile state? The inability to anticipate, and then to deal humanely with the largest exodus of people in India since Partition, was another spectacular failure of public solidarity.

In fact, we saw the very opposite of solidarity. People who supported the lockdown and coercive measures to enforce it—including banning of interstate travel—demanded and were allowed exemptions. Not only did governments give exemptions, they arranged special flights for the affluent who were stuck, not stranded, abroad or at pilgrim sites, and for students forced to confine themselves to their comfortable rented flats and hostel rooms. How radical, redeeming and transformative an act of solidarity it would have been if even a small number of these expatriate professionals, pilgrims and students had refused the special treatment unless the migrant workers desperate to reach their homes were also provided the same assistance and relief.

And then in our fear of the virus, it was as though we needed to find some scapegoat for our fears and hate. The first were people from North-East India, whom we savaged with our apartheid, only because their narrower eyes reminded us racist 'mainlanders' of China, where the virus originated. Many North-Eastern Indians were taunted, shunned, not allowed into stores and neighbourhoods. Then the scapegoat became any outsider. We received reports from around the country where not just gated colonies but poor neighbourhoods and villages too blockaded themselves, with no stranger allowed in, even if hungry and desperate to reach his or her home.

The biggest scapegoat became, as we have seen, the Muslim. Social media was fevered with hate, accusing

Muslims of waging a 'corona jihad', labelling them 'corona bombs'. Social and economic boycotts of Muslims continue to this day.

In these dark, depleting times, legal philosopher Upendra Baxi still suggests the possibility of hope. He writes, 'If the spread of a global pandemic was an act of misfortune, its catastrophisation has to be located in the injustices of social structure and policy. On the other side, the spectacular emergence of new communities of belonging (social groups trying to meet the many needs of migrants on the move), which counter the politics of creating communities of danger, hopefully will become a post-COVID-19 future, ending forever the production of social indifference.'[287] Arundhati Roy also writes of the pandemic as 'a portal, a gateway between one world and the next. We can choose to walk through it, dragging the carcasses of our prejudice and hatred, our avarice, our data banks and dead ideas, our dead rivers and smoky skies behind us. Or we can walk through lightly, with little luggage, ready to imagine another world. And ready to fight for it.'[288]

India has lived too long with inequalities which should be intolerable. Can we now resolve to fight to *build back better*? Can we use the moment of this unprecedented crisis to rebuild our broken country into one which is more compassionate, more just and more equal?

The pandemic demands the best from us. The only chance we have of overcoming it one day is by cementing our solidarity. By holding each other in circles of kindness, across all our differences of class, ethnicity, religion, gender, age and national boundaries. By never turning our faces away; by standing with each other, and with our planet; by caring about and caring for each other.

Acknowledgements

Much gratitude to my colleagues at the Centre for Equity Studies (CES) for their extensive research support: Anirban Bhattacharya, Amitanshu Verma, Mihika Chanchani, Varna Balakrishnan, Balu Sunil, Jenny Sulfath, Misbah Rashid, Banojyotsna, Madhurima Majumder, Sajid Ali, Suresh Garimella, Sagar SK and Shirin Choudhary. Also to Sandeep Yadav for his powerful and moving photographs included in the book.

Notes

1. Lalwani, V. & Sharma, S., 'Watch: In Delhi, hungry people join a 2-km-long food queue in peak afternoon sun.' *Scroll*, 18 April 2020.
2. Mander, H., 'State's measures to fight coronavirus are stripping the poor of dignity and hope.' *Indian Express*, 27 March 2020.
3. National Statistical Organisation. (2014) 'Nutritional Intake in India, 2011-12 NSS 68th Round (JULY 2011—JUNE 2012)' Government of India, Ministry of Statistics and Programme Implementation. October 2014.
4. Boga, D., 'Why malnutrition is growing in rising, urban India', *Business Standard India*, 3 June 2015.
5. Sethi, V., Wagt, A. de, Bhanot, A., Singh, K.D., Agarwal, P., Murira, Z., Bhatia, S., Baswal, D., Unisa, S. & Subramanian, S.V., 'Levels and determinants of malnutrition among India's urban poor women: An analysis of Demographic Health Surveys 2006 and 2016', *Maternal & Child Nutrition*, 16, e12978.
6. 'Top Medical Professionals Call Out Government's "Incoherent" COVID Policy, Lockdown.' *The Wire*, 31 May 2020.
7. 'Census of India Website: Office of the Registrar General & Census Commissioner, India' (2011). Available at: https://censusindia.gov.in/2011census/hh-series/hh01.html
8. Das, B. and Mistri, A. (2013) 'Household quality of living in Indian states: analysis of 2011 census. Environment and Urbanization Asia', 4(1), pp.151-171.
9. Garimella, S & Sunilraj, B., 'In India, migrant labourers bear the brunt of informality, government apathy, and lockdown.' *The People's Dispatch*, 26 April 2020.
10. Ronak Chhabra, 'Locked Down in Crammed Rooms, Residents of Virus-Hit Kapashera Fear the Worst.' Newsclick, 6 May 2020.

11. Das, P.K., 'Sustainable Housing Can't Slip Under the Radar Once the COVID-19 Crisis Subsides.' *The Wire*, 22 April 2020.
12. Raman, V.R; Bora, N. and Singh, K., 'When Covid Hits Slums.' *The Indian Express*, 15 May 2020.
13. Indorewala, H & Wagh, S., 'After the Pandemic, Will We Rethink How We Plan Our Cities?' *The Wire*, 30 April 2020.
14. Chakrabarti, A, 'Study shows you are 4 times more likely to catch coronavirus indoors than outside.' *The Print*, 4 May 2020.
15. Srinivasan, K, 'Lockdown protects the well-off, but what about those who face hunger, homelessness or poor health?'. The Hindu, 18 April 2020.
16. Chakrabarti, P., 'Covid-19 and the Spectres of Colonialism' (2020) *The India Forum*, 14 July 2020.
17. 'ICRA Research' (2020). Available at: https://www.icraresearch.in/research/ViewResearchReport/3117
18. Nanda, P.K., 'Rural joblessness rate up for second straight week', *Livemint*, 28 July 2020.
19. 'More needs to be done to save MSMES and a 100 million jobs.' *The New Indian Express*, 30 July 2020.
20. Darby, L., 'How Are Rich People Getting Richer During the Pandemic?' *GQ*, 28 April 2020.
21. PTI, 'COVID-19 is not health emergency, no need to panic: Health Ministry'. The Hindu, 13 March 2020.
22. Chakravarty, I., 'Across India, lockdown forced women to make perilous journeys home. Some never made it.' *Scroll*, 30 May 2020.
23. Chisti, S., 'Explained: How many migrant workers displaced? A range of estimates.' *The Indian Express*, 8 June 2020.
24. Chisti, S., 'Explained: How many migrant workers displaced? A range of estimates.' *The Indian Express*, 8 June 2020.
25. Agarwal, K., 'Coronavirus Lockdown: As Hunger Grows, the Fear of Starvation Is Real' *The Wire*, 16 April 2020.

26. Reuters, 'No way back: Migrant workers shun city jobs after lockdown ordeal.' *India Today*, 28 May 2020.
27. Nair, S., 'Someone said why not just step out and die of corona, at least we will be counted somewhere.' *The Indian Express*. 1 May 2020.
28. Bordia, R., 'Ground Report: Why Migrants Think They Are Being Held Captive at Delhi Shelter Homes.' *The Wire*, 21 May 2020.
29. Chakravarty, I., 'Across India, lockdown forced women to make perilous journeys home. Some never made it.' *Scroll*, 30 May 2020.
30. Mishra, Sohit, 'Pregnant Woman, Mother Carrying 2 Children—Long Walk Home Amid Lockdown.' NDTV, 6 May 2020.
31. Soutik, B., 'Coronavirus: India's pandemic lockdown turns into a human tragedy.' *BBC News*, 30 March 2020.
32. Jagga, R., 'We walked 600 km on foot, nobody even offered us water.' *The Indian Express*, 18 May 2020.
33. Chakravarty, I., 'A story of swollen feet: The physical toll of walking home during lockdown.' *Scroll*, 14 June 2020.
34. Thakur, P and Painkra, K., 'Jamlo's last journey along a locked-down road.' PARI, 14 May 2020.
35. Peer, B., 'A Friendship, a Pandemic, and a Death Beside a Highway.' *New York Times*, 31 July 2020.
36. PTI, 'About 200 migrant workers lost lives in road accidents during lockdown: Save LIFE Foundation.' *The Economic Times*, 2 June 2020.
37. Chakravarty, I., 'A story of swollen feet: The physical toll of walking home during lockdown'. *Scroll*, 14 June 2020.
38. Special Correspondent, '"Bicycle Girl" Jyoti turns down offer from Cycling Federation', *The Hindu*, 26 May 2020.
39. Chakravarty, I., 'A story of swollen feet: The physical toll of walking home during lockdown.' *Scroll*, 14 June 2020.
40. Bhardwaj, A & Bedi, 'Kejriwal's minister's complaint led to Modi govt action against top Delhi civil servants.' *The Print*, 1 April 2020.

41. Srinivas, R., 'Police beat up migrant workers, send them to shelter homes later.' *The Hindu*, 16 May 2020.
42. Pandey, N., 'With just biscuits and water, migrants on highways walk, cycle to homes hundreds of miles away' *The Print.*,29 April 2020.
43. Salman Ravi's interview with migrants passing through Delhi, available at: https://www.bbc.com/news/av/world-asia-india-52684569/india-migrants-we-will-die-we-are-poor-people
44. Mander, H., 'For India's migrant workers, the prospect of life with dignity has become more remote.' *Scroll*, 5 May 2020.
45. Johari, A., '"I can't even express my anger": Confusion reigns as migrant workers in Mumbai struggle to get home.' *Scroll*, 5 May 2020.
46. Kumar, A., 'Denied entry into state by district admin, thousands of hungry, helpless migrants stuck at UP-MP border.' *India Today*, 10 May 2020.
47. Rashid, O., 'UP sends buses to bring students back from Kota.' *The Hindu*, 17 April 2020.
48. Rashid, O., 'UP sends buses to bring students back from Kota.' *The Hindu*, 17 April 2020
49. Mohan, P. & Amin, A., 'Forcing migrants to stay back in cities amid lockdown worsened the Covid-19 spread,' Scroll, 3 June 2020.
50. Johari, A., '"I can't even express my anger": Confusion reigns as migrant workers in Mumbai struggle to get home' *Scroll*, 5 May 2020.
51. Siddique, I & Waghmode, V., 'Train lottery leaves migrants in lurch: "When will my turn come?"' *The Indian Express*, 17 May 2020.
52. Sharma, S., 'They walk 30 km. Wait four days for a train. No one's told them they're at the wrong station' *Scroll*, 16 May 2020.
53. Johari, A., '"I can't even express my anger": Confusion reigns as migrant workers in Mumbai struggle to get home' *Scroll.* 5th May 2020.

54. Sharma, S., 'They walk 30 km. Wait four days for a train. No one's told them they're at the wrong station' *Scroll*, 16 May 2020.
55. Srivastava, S., 'Far from subsidising Shramik trains, Modi government is actually charging extra for them' *Scroll*, 12 June 2020.
56. Dhingra, S., 'Modi government finally clarifies it's not paying Shramik Express fare.' *The Print*, 28 May 2020.
57. Mishra, D., सुप्रीम कोर्ट के आदेश का उल्लंघन करते हुए रेलवे ने श्रमिकों से वसूला करोड़ों रुपये किराया,' *The Wire Hindi*, 3 September 2020.
58. Jain, B., 'Inter-state movement relaxation only for stranded migrants: MHA' *Times of India*. 3 May 2020.
59. Shivakumar, C., 'TN bid to kickstart economy may run into manpower crisis as migrants prefer to return home' *New Indian Express*. 2 May 2020.
60. Dutta, A., 'Railway Protection Force reports 80 deaths on Shramik trains.' *Hindustan Times*, 30 May 2020.
61. Haksar, N., 'Filthy toilets, attacked with stones: For North East workers from Goa, a 119-hour nightmare on rails.' *Scroll*, 27 May 2020.
62. Butani, A & Tiwari, A., 'Question facing migrants: Stay home or return?' *Indian Express*, 19 June 2020.
63. Shah, A, & Lerche, J., 'The five truths about the migrant workers' crisis.' *Hindustan Times*, 13 July 2020.
64. 'After the long marches: What do workers want?—Working Peoples Charter' 31 August, Available at: https://workingpeoplescharter.in/media-statements/after-long-marches-what-do-workers-want/
65. Srivastava, R & Nagaraj, A., 'No Way Back: Indian workers shun city jobs after lockdown ordeal.' Thomson Reuters Foundation News, 28 May 2020.
66. Srivastava, R & Nagaraj, A., 'No Way Back: Indian workers shun city jobs after lockdown ordeal.' Thomson Reuters Foundation News, 28 May 2020.
67. Ghose, D., 'First Covid, now hunger, Bhagalpur migrants start packing—again.' *The Indian Express*, 28 June 2020.

68. Budhwar, N., 'Between one home and another, the pandemic lays it bare'. 25 October 2020.

69. Chakravarty, I., 'Across India, lockdown forced women to make perilous journeys home. Some never made it' *Scroll.* 30 May 2020.

70. Ghose, D. (2020) 'As a district unlocks: "Left on a truck to see family, but now I am returning to save them"' *The Indian Express*, 27 July 2020.

71. Sumner, A,. Eduardo Ortiz-Juarez, E.& Hoy, C. (2020) 'Precarity and the pandemic: COVID-19 and poverty incidence, intensity, and severity in developing countries', *WIDER Working Paper 2020/77*, United Nations University-Wider.

72. Mohanty, P., 'Rebooting Economy VIII: COVID-19 pandemic could push millions of Indians into poverty and hunger.' *Business Today*, 20 July 2020.

73. Pothan, E., 'Local food systems and COVID-19; A glimpse on India's responses.' *Food and Agricultural Organisation of the United Nations*, 22 April 2020.

74. SWAN, '21 Days and Counting: COVID-19 Lockdown, Migrant Workers, and the Inadequacy of Welfare Measures in India.' Available at: https://www.thehindu.com/news/resources/article31442220.ece/binary/Lockdown-and-Distress_Report-by-Stranded-Workers-Action-Network.pdf

75. Agarwal, K., 'Coronavirus Lockdown: As Hunger Grows, the Fear of Starvation Is Real' *The Wire*, 16 April 2020.

76. Patnaik, P., 'Two Basic Lessons from the Coronavirus Pandemic.' *NewsClick*, 20 March 2020.

77. National Commission for Enterprises in the Unorganized Sector (2007). Report on the Conditions of Work and Promotion of Livelihoods in the Unorganized Sector. New Delhi: Government of India. Source: Aajeevika Bureau—'Unlocking the Urban' Report.

78. Harris-White, B., 'The Modi Sarkar's Project for India's Informal Economy' *The Wire*. 20 May 2020.

79. Patnaik, P., Ghosh, J. & Mander, H., 'Covid-19 crisis calls

for universal delivery of food and cash transfers by the state' *The Indian Express*, 27 April 2020.

80. Standing Committee on Labour (2011) Inter-State Migrant Working Report. Available at: https://www.prsindia.org/sites/default/files/bill_files/SCR_Inter_State_Migrant_Workment_Bill_2011.pdf
81. Sulfath, J & Sunilraj, B., 'Covid 19 Crisis Exposes Indian's Neglect of Informal Workers' *NewsClick*, 13 May 2020.
82. Department of Labour, Karnataka Report. Available at https://www.labour.karnataka.gov.in/storage/pdf-files/2018-19/Annual%20Report%202018-19%20English%20report.pdf
83. Tiwari, S., 'No Documents, No Benefits: How India's Invisible Workforce Is Left to Fend For Itself.' *IndiaSpend*, 21 June 2020.
84. 'Parliamentary panel seeks clarification from nine states including UP and Gujarat on dilution of labour laws.' *New Indian Express*, 13 May 2020.
85. Gaur, V., 'Uttar Pradesh brings ordinance to suspend most labour laws for 3 years.' *The Economic Times*, 7 May 2020.
86. 'The Government of Madhya Pradesh provides certain relaxation to factories registered under the Factories Act.' *Legality Simplified*, 29 April 2020.
87. Balasubramanyam, K., 'Karnataka to join new labour league, to amend labour laws to bail out industrial sector'. *The Economic Times*. 12 May 2020.
88. 'MP 05 05 2020 Amendment to Labour Laws.pdf' *Google Docs*. Available at: https://drive.google.com/file/d/1sRY2Neeva6htnaF2Kq2FsyuCRWgFLA_m/view?usp=embed_facebook
89. 'Industrial Disputes Act, 1947 | Bare Acts | Law Library | AdvocateKhoj' Available at: https://www.advocatekhoj.com/library/bareacts/industrial/index.php?Title=Industrial%20Disputes%20Act,%201947
90. 'MP 05 05 2020 Amendment to Labour Laws.pdf' *Google Docs*. Available at: https://drive.google.com/file/d/1sRY2Ne

eva6htnaF2Kq2FsyuCRWgFLA_m/view?usp=embed_facebook

91. 'M.P. Industrial Relations Act, 1960.' Available at: http://bareactslive.com/MP/MP333.HTM
92. Information and Public Relations Department, Uttar Pradesh (2020) '6/7 press note.pdf—Google Drive' Available at: https://drive.google.com/file/d/1cwpaqzYaWBt_I_7U2rusRJ0qZZ8yQiDe/view
93. CMO Gujarat on Twitter: "In order to boost economic activities and generate employment in the post-lockdown period in Gujarat, CM Shri @vijayrupanibjp announces exemption for new industrial projects from Labour Laws except provisions for minimum wages, safety and compensation in case of accidents. https://t.co/8UkHH0gtX5" / Twitter' *Twitter*. Available at: https://twitter.com/CMOGuj/status/ 1258766075786694656
94. Available at: https://twitter.com/AnoopSatpathy/status/1258790301679960067
95. ' 11/4 factory worker.pdf' (2020) *Google Docs*. Available at: https://drive.google.com/file/d/1U3QfvpnVGpEnsKfXewApxre2PxUUhpH2/view?usp=embed_facebook
96. 'Vini Mahajan on Twitter: "https://t.co/F3DGq7BxTm" / Twitter' *Twitter*. Available at: https://twitter.com/mahajan_vini/status/1252163789480394752
97. PTI, 'Punjab mulls changes in labour laws, excise policy' *Business Insider*, 8 May 2020.
98. Shah, A, & Lerche, J., 'The five truths about the migrant workers' crisis.' *Hindustan Times*, 13 July 2020.
99. Roy, D., '"No Other Way": Full Text Of PM Modi's Speech Announcing Lockdown.' *NDTV.com.* 24 March 2020.
100. Dhingra, S., 'Don't cut salaries or fire workers during lockdown—Modi govt issues advisory.' *The Print.* March 23 2020.
101. ET Bureau, 'Nirmala Sitharaman announcements: FM Nirmala Sitharaman announces Rs 1.7 lakh crore relief package for poor' *The Economic Times* 27 March 2020.

102. HT Correspondent, 'Mann ki Baat: "Diseases must be dealt with at the very beginning," says PM Modi on Covid-19.' *Hindustan Times*, 29 May 2020.
103. 'In Letter to Country, Modi Speaks of "Tremendous Suffering" of Migrants in Battle Against Coronavirus.' Ne*ws18*, 30 May 2020.
104. The Wire Staff, 'PM Extends Free Ration Scheme till Nov: Experts Cite Food Surplus, Cloud Remains Over Migrants.' *The Wire*, 30 June 2020.
105. Sharma, H., 'Only 13% of allocated free food grain handed out to returning migrant workers, reveals govt data.' *The Indian Express*, 2 July 2020.
106. Agarwal, K., 'Coronavirus lockdown: As hunger grows, the fear of starvation is real.' *The Wire*, 16 April 2020.
107. Rajagopalan, S., 'India needs Jan Dhan, and not just Jan Dhan accounts', *Livemint*, 29 May 2018.
108. Anand, U., 'No Need for Migrants to Go Back to Hometown, Centre Tells SC, Warns of Serious Health Hazard' 27 April 2020.
109. Anand, U., 'No Need for Migrants to Go Back to Hometown, Centre Tells SC, Warns of Serious Health Hazard' 27 April 2020.
110. 'Around 21,500 relief camps set up for migrant workers, more than 6.75 lakh persons being provided shelter, around 25 lakh being provided meals: Union Home Ministry.' PIB, 1 April 2020. Available at: https://pib.gov.in/PressReleseDetail.aspx?PRID=1609954
111. Correspondent, Legal, 'Coronavirus Centre files report on migrant workers.' *The Hindu*, 7 April 2020.
112. Rajan, S.I. (2014), *Social Security for the Elderly: Experiences from South Asia*, Routledge.
113. Mander, H, 'Harsh Mander: For India's migrant workers, the prospect of life with dignity has become more remote' 5 May 2020.
114. Mander, H (2020). 'Harsh Mander: For India's migrant workers, the prospect of life with dignity has become more remote' 5 May 2020.

115. 'Modi's Rs 20 Lakh Crore Package Will Likely Have Fiscal Cost of Less Than Rs 2.5 Lakh Crore.' *The Wire*, 17 May 2020.
116. Marwah, N., 'The PM of India is the only Leader out of 200+ Countries Affected by Coronavirus in this World Who Did Not Face the Press during these Turbulent Times!', *Inventiva*. 12 June 2020. .
117. Sakar, R., 'New Zealand: No new COVID-19 cases for 15 days.' 6 June 2020.
118. Cousins, S., 'New Zealand eliminates COVID-19.' *The Lancet*, 395(10235), p. 1474. doi: 10.1016/S0140-6736(20) 31097-7.
119. Chakravarty, I., '"Fake news" did not trigger India's worst migrant crisis. Government apathy did.' *Scroll*, 27 September 2020.
120. 'SWAN, *21 Days and Counting: COVID-19 Lockdown, Migrant Workers, and the Inadequacy of Welfare Measures in Inda*' *The Hindu,* 15 April 2020
121. Bhushan, P., 'The Supreme Court Is Locked Down and Justice Is in "Emergency" Care.' *The Wire,* 28 April 2020.
122. Nair, S., 'Pandemic, distress, a broken phone.' *The Indian Express*, 23 October 2020.
123. Baxi, U., 'Exodus Constitutionalism.' *The India Forum*. 29 June 2020.
124. Das, S., 'An estimation of required fiscal stimulus to revive the economy in India.' *VIKALP*, 6 May 2020.
125. Kanitkar, T., 'Why India's Covid-19 Package is Grossly Inadequate.' *NewsClick*, 2 April 2020.
126. Jha, P.S., 'India Needs a Big-Bang Stimulus, Not Sermons on How There Is No Free Lunch.' *The Wire*, 12 May 2020.
127. Mulye, P., 'The coronavirus crisis may prove to be a "mass-extinction event" for India's small businesses', *Scroll*, 28 July 2020.
128. Thomas, C., 'In Indian cities, home-based workers are being paid Rs 15 for a day's work since the lockdown.' *Scroll*, 28 July 2020.

129. Rukmini, S., 'How covid-19 locked out women from jobs.' *Mint*, 11 June 2020.
130. The Wire Analysis. 'What Job Losses in the Formal Sector Tell Us About the Lockdown's Impact on Economy.' *The Wire*, 19 August 2020.
131. Thomas, J.J., 'India's poor may have lost Rs 4 lakh crore in the coronavirus lockdown', *Scroll*, 4 June 2020.
132. Kannan, K.P., 'COVID-19 Lockdown: Protecting the Poor Means Keeping the Indian Economy Afloat.' *Economic and Political Weekly*, 3 April 2020.
133. 'During lockdown, rural India faced insurmountable sufferings; 74% satisfied with government.' *Gaonconnection | Your Connection with Rural India*, 10 August 2020.
134. Scroll Staff, 'In charts: India's GDP shrinks more than other major economies, decline set in before pandemic.' *Scroll*, 2 September 2020.
135. Scroll Staff, 'In charts: India's GDP shrinks more than other major economies, decline set in before pandemic.' *Scroll*, 2 September 2020.
136. ENS Bureau, 'Minus 23.9 per cent.' *The Indian Express*, 1 September 2020.
137. 'SA Aiyar Blog.' *Times of India Blog*, 14 June 2020.
138. Sonwalkar, P., 'Covid-19 could kill more through hunger, 122 million more may be pushed to starvation: Oxfam' *Hindustan Times*. 9 July 2020.
139. 'UNICEF—Humanitarian Action for Children—Coronavirus (COVID-19) Global Response.' Available at: https://www.unicef.org/appeals/covid-2019.html
140. Bordia, R., 'Hunger and malnutrition loom large over India as anganwadis stay shut amid coronavirus pandemic', *Scroll*, 11 September 2020.
141. Dutt, A., 'With regular services shut, many hospitals turn away non-Covid patients.' *Hindustan Times*, 11 May 2020.
142. PTI, 'State hospitals in Mumbai subject non-COVID-19 patients to long waits.' *Moneycontrol.com* 19 May 2020.
143. Jayachandran, N., 'Non-COVID-19 patients in Bengaluru

are scrambling to avail treatment amid lockdown.' *The News Minute*, 3 May 2020.

144. Cash, R. & Patel, V., 'Has COVID-19 subverted global health?' *The Lancet*, 5 May 2020.
145. Sharma, S., 'India records 41% dip in annual malaria deaths: WHO's report.' *Hindustan Times*, 4 December 2019.
146. TNN, 'These diseases kill many more than coronavirus.' *The Times of India*, 17 March 2020.
147. Tiemersma, E.W., van der Werf, M.J., Borgdorff, M.W., Williams, B.G. & Nagelkerke, N.J.D. (2011) 'Natural History of Tuberculosis: Duration and Fatality of Untreated Pulmonary Tuberculosis in HIV Negative Patients: A Systematic Review', *PLoS ONE*, 6.
148. Bloom, B.R., Atun, R., Cohen, T., Dye, C., Fraser, H., Gomez, G.B., Knight, G., Murray, M., Nardell, E., Rubin, E., Salomon, J., Vassall, A., Volchenkov, G., White, R., Wilson, D. & Yadav, P. (2017) 'Tuberculosis', in Holmes, K. K., Bertozzi, S., Bloom, B. R., and Jha, P. (eds) *Major Infectious Diseases. 3rd ed., Washington (DC): The International Bank for Reconstruction and Development / The World Bank.*
149. *The Potential Impact of the COVID-19 Response on Tuberculosis in High-burden countries: A Modelling Analysis.* Available at: http://www.stoptb.org/assets/documents/news/Modeling%20Report_1%20May%202020_FINAL.pdf
150. FRHS India, *Impact of COVID 19 on India's Family Planning Program*. Available at: http://www.frhsi.org.in/images/impact-of-covid-19-on-indias-family-planning-program-policy-brief.pdf
151. Rukmini, S., 'COVID-19 Disrupted India's Routine Health Services.' *IndiaSpend*, 27 August 2020.
152. 'Coronavirus pandemic: Mental illness cases rise in India after COVID-19 outbreak' *Moneycontrol.com* 14 April 2020.
153. Joy, S., 'Coronavirus Crisis: No lockdown for domestic violence.' *Deccan Herald*, 26 April 2020.
154. Naik, A., 'As India's lockdown ends, a mental health crisis is looming.' *World Economic Forum*, 18 May 2020.

155. Yadav, P.N., 'COVID-19 Lockdown May Have Debilitating Effect On Alcoholics, Drug Addicts, Those In Rehab: Psychiatrists' *https://www.outlookindia.com/*. 1 April 2020.
156. George, C., '"Humanity is greater than religion…my father's coffin was buried by a Muslim, a Hindu and two others"' *The Indian Express*, 16 June 2020.
157. Sharma, S., 'Millions of children may be pushed to work due to Covid-19.' *Hindustan Times*, 13 June 2020.
158. 'Children in Distress.' Indian Express (Editorial), 16 October 2020.
159. 'COVID-19: Centre blames Tablighi Jamaat for sudden spike in cases.' *The Week*, 1 April 2020.
160. Jain, R., 'How India's Government Set off a Spiral of Islamophobia.' 20 April 2020.
161. 'After Minority Commission's Intervention, Delhi Govt. Stops Mentioning Tablighi Markaz in Coronavirus Bulletins', *IndiaTomorrow.net*, 11 April 2020.
162. Daniyal, S., 'Explained: Sampling bias drove sensationalist reporting around Tablighi coronavirus cases', *Scroll.in*, 7 April 2020.
163. Media Watcher, 'Fracas over Tablighi Jamaat.' *National Herald*, 1 April 2020.
164. 'Defying lockdown, devotees in Bengal assemble at temples on Ram Navami.' *The Hindu*, 2 April 2020.
165. Statesman News Service Web Desk, 'Hundreds violate lockdown order in Karnataka to participate in temple event.' *The Statesman*, 17 April 2020.
166. Patel, J. and Zubair, M., 'Video of Muslim vendor's unhygienic handling of fruits falsely linked with spreading coronavirus', *Alt News*, 4 April 2020.
167. Roy, S., 'Hate Goes Viral in India.' *The Diplomat*, 4 May.
168. Chakravarty, S. & Iyer, S., 'Tablighi Jamaat: Impact of media narratives', *Hindu Businessline*, 7 August 2020.
169. 'Tablighi Jamaat, the human bomb which can explode Coronavirus numbers | Master Stroke.' Available at: https://news.abplive.com/tv-show/master-stroke/tablighi-jamaat-

the-human-bomb-which-can-explode-coronavirus-numbers- master-stroke-31032020-1186329

170. 'DNA: Tablighi Jamaat Betrayed the Nation?' Available at: https://zeenews.india.com/video/india/dna-tablighi-jamaat-betrayed-the-nation-2273020.html
171. PTI, 'Tablighi returnees from Delhi are like human bombs: Former Maharashtra CM Devendra Fadnavis' *The New Indian Express*, 8 April 2020.
172. Iyer, A., '"Minds Have Been Poisoned": HP Villagers on Attack on J&K Workers.' *The Quint*, 17 April 2020.
173. Saikia, A., 'The other virus: Hate crimes against India's Muslims are spreading with Covid-19.' Scroll.in, 8 April 2020.
174. Ara, I., 'Mosque Vandalised in Mukhmelpur Near Delhi, Locals Claim, Police Deny.' *The Wire*, 5 April 2020.
175. 'Two Muslim men attacked in Karnataka's Bagalkot, accused of spreading COVID-19.' Times Now. Available at: https://www.youtube.com/watch?v=auzwO6Fex2s.
176. Jain, R., 'How India's Government Set off a Spiral of Islamophobia.' 20 April 2020.
177. *Prime Time With Ravish Kumar: Foreigners Made 'Scapegoat' Over Covid: Court On Islamic Sect Event*. Available at: https://www.youtube.com/watch?v=fj_RnDbilYE
178. Bhattacharya, A. & Ali, S., 'Shamsher Ali and Sons: Peeling the Layers of Struggle that Define Lockdown for One Family' *The Wire*, 24 April 2020.
179. Singh, P., 'Punjab: Muslim Gujjar Families "Beaten and Boycotted" in Hoshiarpur Villages.' *The Wire*, 7 April 2020.
180. Arora, K., 'Post Lockdown, Social Boycott of Gujjars Continues in Punjab Village.' *The Wire*, 24 June 2020.
181. Trivedi, D., 'Targeting a community.' *Frontline*, 8 May 2020.
182. Singh, R.K., & Raju, S., 'Ahead of Eid, UP releases over 600 Tablighi Jamaat members from quarantine.' *Hindustan Times*, 21 May 2020.
183. Jafri, A.A., 'A Black Eid for Tablighi Jamaatis? No Release of

Quarantined Men Even After 45 Days.' *NewsClick*, 19 May 2020.

184. Thapar, A. & Wahidi, Z., '"Unjust and unfair": What three High Courts said about the arrests of Tablighi Jamaat members.' *Scroll*, 24 August 2020.
185. Venugopal, V., 'Tablighi Jamaat is a Talibani crime, not negligence: Mukhtar Abbas Naqvi—The Economic Times.' *The Economic Times*, 2 April 2020.
186. Nigam, A., '"46% Muslims in urban India self-employed".' *Bussiness Line*, 9 August 2020.
187. Thapar, A. & Wahidi, Z., '"Unjust and unfair": What three High Courts said about the arrests of Tablighi Jamaat members.' *Scroll*, 24 August 2020.
188. Deutsche Welle, 'Yuval Noah Harari, on Hatred that Poses a Bigger Danger Than the Virus Itself' *The Wire*. 24 April 2020.
189. Ramani, P., 'Coronavirus: This Tablighi From Djibouti Still Loves India.' Bloombergquint, 26 August 2020.
190. Balkrishnan, V. and Vishwnathan, M., 'Scroll.in—Delhi riots: The violence has left a mental health crisis that will last generations.' *Maninblue1947's Weblog*, 18 Augus 2020.
191. Rajagopal, K., 'Coronavirus | SC notice to States on parole to those facing up to 7-year term.' *The Hindu*, 23 March 2020.
192. Khaitan, N. and Khanna, M., 'Opinion | Rampant arrests in time of lockdown.' *The Hindu*, 22 April 2020.
193. Khan, F., 'Minorities panel notice to Delhi Police for "random" arrests of Muslims every day for riots.' *ThePrint*, 6 April 2020.
194. Bhandari, H., 'Delhi riots: "25-30 arrests from north-east since lockdown".' *The Hindu*, 17 April 2020.
195. Manral, M.S., 'NE Delhi riots: 800 arrests made as MHA intervenes.' *The Indian Express*, 13 April 2020.
196. Iyer, A. S., 'Under Lockdown, Confusion & Fear Grip NE Delhi As Arrests Increase.' *The Quint*, 22 April 2020.
197. Manral, M. S., 'NE Delhi riots: 800 arrests made as MHA intervenes.' *The Indian Express*, 13 April 2020.

198. Misra, U. and Iqbal, N., 'Heart of Darkness: The context of violence in Northeast Delhi, India's most densely populated district | Cities News.' *The Indian Express*, 1 March 2020.

199. Pillai, V., 'India is scaling up health infrastructure, has 1 lakh beds for COVID-19 patients, says PM Modi.' *Moneycontrol.com* 14 April 2020.

200. Sawant, S. & Dubey, N., 'Exclusive: Cancer patient who was shifted by BMC to live "under Hindmata bridge" dies.' *Mumbai Live*. April 2020.

201. Siddique, I., 'Delhi: Coaches too hot for patients, Railways looks for solutions—and some rain.' *MSN*, 20 June 2020.

202. Kumar, K., 'Mumbai staring at a huge shortage of doctors and health professionals.' *The Economic Times*, 7 May 2020.

203. Babu, N.M., 'Virus patient dies, kin allege hospitals refused admission.' *The Hindu*, 5 June 2020.

204. Yadav, S., 'Refused care in Delhi, COVID-19 patient travels 700 km by rail, dies in hometown.' *The Hindu*, 9 June 2020.

205. Ellis-Petersen, H. & Dhillon, A., (2020) 'India's coronavirus agony: "I did everything to save my wife and baby".' *The Guardian*, 12 June 2020.

206. Scroll Staff, 'Coronavirus: Mother, newborns die in Dehradun after four hospitals refuse treatment, inquiry ordered', *Scroll*, 13 June 2020.

207. 'India running out of hospital beds amid record coronavirus cases.' A*ljazeera.com* 9 June 2020.

208. Lalwani, V., 'A visit to two Covid hospitals in Delhi reveals a nightmare for patients and their families.' *Scroll.in*, 17 June 2020.

209. Johari, A., 'In Mumbai, Covid-19 patients are dying as they wait for ambulances and hospital beds', *Scroll*, 4 June 2020.

210. AFP, 'Monkeys steal Covid-19 test samples from health worker in India.' *The Guardian* 29 May 2020.

211. Staff Reporter, 'Coronavirus: 35 people in Noida sent to isolation ward after private lab mixes up test results.' *Scroll*, 11 June 2020.

212. Patel, S., 'Delhi: Family buries the wrong body after mix-up at Lok Nayak mortuary.' *The Indian Express*, 8 June 2020.
213. Didiyala, A., 'Second mix-up in 3 days at Gandhi Hospital, family gets wrong body, buries it.' *Times of India* 12 June 2020.
214. Ananthakrishnan, G., 'Deplorable, pathetic: SC slams Delhi, says state duty-bound to provide care.' *The Indian Express*, 13 June 2020.
215. Singh, S., 'Surviving COVID-19, a Fire, 2 Hospitals and a Struggling System: A Patient Speaks.' *The Wire*. 16 June 2020.
216. Sethi, N. & Shrivastava, K., 'Frustration in National Covid-19 Task Force.' *Article 14,* 24 April 2020.
217. Koshy, J., 'Coronavirus | In February, ICMR scientists doubted efficacy of lockdown.' *The Hindu*, 9 April 2020.
218. Krishnan, V., 'Modi administration did not consult ICMR-appointed COVID task force before key decisions.' *The Caravan*, 15 April 2020.
219. Konikkara, A. & Krishnan, V., 'Members of PM's COVID-19 task force say lockdown failed due to unscientific implementation.' *The Caravan*, 19 May 2020.
220. Baxi, U., 'Exodus Constitutionalism.' *The India Forum*, 29 June 2020.
221. Deepankar, B., 'India's COVID-19 testing conundrum.' *The Wire Science*, 27 April 2020.
222. 'WHO chief scientist says India's testing rate is very low compared to many other countries.' *Scroll*, 4 August 2020.
223. Sethi, N. & Shrivastava, Kumar S., 'Govt Knew Lockdown Would Delay, Not Control Pandemic.' *Article 14*, 23 April 2020.
224. Konikkara, A. & Krishnan, V., 'Members of PM's COVID-19 task force say lockdown failed due to unscientific implementation.' *The Caravan*, 19 May 2020.
225. Krishnan, V., 'India did not stockpile COVID protective equipment for health workers despite clear WHO guidelines.' *The Caravan*, 22 March 2020.

226. Konikkara, A. & Krishnan, V., 'Members of PM's COVID-19 task force say lockdown failed due to unscientific implementation.' *The Caravan*, 19 May 2020.
227. Konikkara, A. & Krishnan, V., 'Members of PM's COVID-19 task force say lockdown failed due to unscientific implementation.' *The Caravan*, 19 May 2020.
228. Leading public health professionals and scholars Vikram Patel, Vandana Prasad, T Sundararaman and Vikas Bajpai, and retired civil servants Sujatha Rao and Keshav Desiraju, who led the public health ministry in the union government, participated in this discussion.
229. Krishnan, V., 'Surge in Covid cases proves centre wrong.' *Caravan*, 7 May 2020.
230. Mahurkar, U., 'Inside PM Modi's COVID-19 Task Force.' 9 April 2020.
231. Venkataramakrishnan, R., 'Why has India stopped health ministry briefings even as Covid-19 cases cross the 1,00,000 mark?' *Scroll*, 20 May 2020.
232. Thacker, T., 'Government to stop daily Covid briefings.' *The Economic Times* 20 May 2020.
233. Venkataramakrishnan, R., 'Why has India stopped health ministry briefings even as Covid-19 cases cross the 1,00,000 mark?' *Scroll*, 20 May 2020.
234. 'Testing Strategy' (2020). Available at: https://www.icmr.gov.in/cteststrat.html
235. Ray, A., 'Delhi govt revised testing guidelines, will test only symptomatic contacts.' *Livemint*. 5 June 2020.
236. Dutt, A & Mishra, A., 'Delhi bars labs "flouting" rules, test capacity dips.' *Hindustan Times*, 5 June 2020.
237. PTI, 'Follow Lieutenant Governor's Order On COVID-19 Testing: High Court To Delhi.' *NDTV.com* 22 June 2020.
238. 'A question of quarantine: On migrant workers and other travellers.' *The Hindu*, 16 May 2020.
239. Express News Service, 'Day after Delhi sealed borders: Now Haryana says borders to open only on mutual consent.' *The Indian Express*, 3 June 2020.

240. Khandelwal, P., 'Lockdown: Day after UP govt's order, migrants on foot stopped at Delhi border by police.' *Hindustan Times*, 17 May 2020.
241. PTI, 'Fear factor combined with fake news creates new "infodemic" on social media.' *The Hindu,* 30 March 2020.
242. Penkar, A., 'Fact Check: The lies and misdirections of the Modi government during the coronavirus lockdown.' *The Caravan*, 13 June 2020.
243. Krishnan, V., 'Gujarat illustrates the Modi government's science denialism during the coronavirus pandemic', *The Caravan*, 23 June 2020.
244. Krishnan, V., 'Delhi HC exposes companies profiteering from COVID antibody test kits; ICMR cancels procurement order.' *The Caravan*, 27 April 2020. Mehrotra, K. (2020) 'Covid-19: ICMR clears first batch of key ELISA antibody testing kits made in India.' *The Indian Express*, 15 May 2020.
245. Menon, S., 'Coronavirus: India is turning to faster tests to meet targets.' BBC, 24 August 2020.
246. Mehrotra, K., 'Glaring gaps in number of testing labs marks next Covid challenge.' *The Indian Express*, 24 May 2020.
247. 'India: COVID-19 test centers by state.' *Statista*. Available at: https://www.statista.com/statistics/1104075/india-coronavirus-covid-19-public-private-testing-centers-by-state/
248. Bordia, R., 'Ground Report: Why Migrants Think They Are Being Held Captive at Delhi Shelter Homes.' *The Wire*, 21 May 2020.
249. Central Bureau of Health Intelligence. *National Health Profile 2019*, 14th issue. Ministry of Health and Family Welfare, Government of India.
250. Krishnan, V., 'Lack of testing kits, understaffed hospitals: COVID exposes India's crumbling healthcare system.' *Caravan*, 16 March 2020.
251. Tiwari, S., '"India spent 1% of GDP on public health for 15 years. Result is vulnerability to crises".' 26 June 2020.

252. Central Bureau of Health Intelligence. *National Health Profile 2019*, 14th issue. Ministry of Health and Family Welfare, Government of India.
253. Tiwari, S., '"India spent 1% of GDP on public health for 15 years. Result is vulnerability to crises".' 26 June 2020.
254. 'Indian healthcare professionals prefer private jobs; study claims gross uneven distribution of healthcare professionals.' *The New Indian Express*, 29 May 2020.
255. Garg, S., Bebarta, K.K. & Tripathi, N., 'Performance of India's national publicly funded health insurance scheme, Pradhan Mantri Jan Arogaya Yojana (PMJAY), in improving access and financial protection for hospital care: findings from household surveys in Chhattisgarh state', *BMC Public Health*, 20, 949.
256. Raghavan, P., Barnagarwala, T. and Ghosh, A., 'Covid fight: Govt system in front, private hospitals do the distancing.' *The Indian Express*, 30 April 2020.
257. Yamunan, S., 'Fear of Covid-19 spread makes private hospitals turn away patients—or charge them higher bills.' *Scroll*, 23 April 2020.
258. Bhuyan, A. and IndiaSpend.com, 'In the middle of a pandemic, Indian hospitals are inflating the cost of even non-coronavirus care.' *Scroll.in*, 7 June 2020.
259. 'HT Chandigarh debate: Don't make patients pay for Covid-19 safety measures.' *Hindustan Times*, 30 May 2020.
260. *Ibid.*
261. Mohanty, P., 'Coronavirus Lockdown XI: Why India's health policy needs a course correction.' *Business Today*, 9 April 2020.
262. McCurry, J, 'Test, trace, contain: how South Korea flattened its coronavirus curve.' *The Guardian* 23 April 2020.
263. Yadavar, S., 'How Covid hotspot Dharavi, Asia's largest slum, fought against all odds to flatten the curve.' *ThecPrint*, 14 June 2020.
264. *Ibid.*
265. '"Chasing the virus": How India's largest slum beat back a pandemic—Raw Story.' Agence France-Presse, 1 July 2020.

266. Patel, V., 'Reputation of scientists will be further muddied by our role in this pandemic.' *The Indian Express*, 30 July 2020.
267. Patel, V., 'Reputation of scientists will be further muddied by our role in this pandemic.' *The Indian Express*, 30 July 2020.
268. Indian Public Health Association (IPHA), Indian Association of Preventive and Social Medicine (IAPSM) and Indian Association of Epidemiologists (2020) *2nd Joint Statement on CoVID-19 Pandemic in India—Public Health Approach for COVID19 Control.* Available at: https://www.iphaonline.org/wp-content/uploads/2020/05/Second-Joint-Statement-of-IPHA-IAPSM-and-IAE-on-COVID-19-containment-plan-May-25-2020_Shorter-version-final.pdf.
269. The Wire Staff, 'Top Medical Professionals Call Out Government's "Incoherent" COVID Policy, Lockdown.' *The Wire*, 31 May 2020.
270. Why India's COVID-19 Outbreak is Now World's Fastest Growing I Karan Thapar I Ashish Jha (2020). Available at: https://www.youtube.com/watch?v=NbuvL2QyxQo
271. Davidson, H., 'Around 20% of global population under coronavirus lockdown.' *The Guardian*, 24 March 2020.
272. *Coronavirus Government Response Tracker, Blavatnik School of Government, University of Oxford.* Available at: https://www.bsg.ox.ac.uk/research/research-projects/coronavirus-government-response-tracker
273. Caduff, C., 'What Went Wrong: Corona and the World after the Full Stop.' Available at: https://www.academia.edu/42829792/What_Went_Wrong_Corona_and_the_World_after_the_Full_Stop
274. WHO, *India: WHO Coronavirus Disease (COVID-19) Dashboard, World Health Organisation.* Available at: https://covid19.who.int/region/searo/country/in
275. 'China expands coronavirus outbreak lockdown to 56 million people.' *Aljazeera* 25 January 2020.
276. Daniyal, S., 'Coronavirus: Why is Pakistan doing so much better than India?', *Scroll*, 11 September 2020.

277. Daniyal, S., 'Coronavirus: Why is Pakistan doing so much better than India?', *Scroll*, 11 September 2020.
278. Aiyar, S.A., 'Phase lockdowns out, give more cash to poor.' *Times of India Blog*, 13 September 2020.
279. Mander, H., Ghosh, J. and Patnaik, P., 'A plan to revive a broken economy.' *The Hindu*, 14 May 2020.
280. India Brand Equity Foundation (2020), *Indian Railways: Network, Investments, Market Size, Govt Initiatives | IBEF, India Brand Equity Foundation*. Available at: https://www.ibef.org/industry/indian-railways.aspx
281. '60 lakh migrants took 4,450 Shramik specials to reach their home States: Railways.' *The Hindu* 15 June 2020.
282. Kumar, S., 'India's economy has suffered even more than most.' *The Economist*, 23 May 2020.
283. Lakhani, S., 'In Defence Colony, Covid positive help made to wait hours for ambulance.' *The Indian Express*, 15 May 2020.
284. 'Live | Facebook' (2020). Available at: https://www.facebook.com/watch/live/?v=1513108172210330&ref=watch_permalink
285. Baxi, U., 'Exodus Constitutionalism.' *The India Forum*, 29 June 2020.
286. Kumar, R., '"When You're Going Through Hell, Keep Going".' *Medium*, 25 June 2020.
287. Baxi, U., 'Exodus Constitutionalism.' *The India Forum*, 29 June 2020.
288. 'Arundhati Roy: "The pandemic is a portal" | Free to read'. Available at: https://www.ft.com/content/10d8f5e8-74eb-11ea-95fe-fcd274e920ca